# THE EXCHANGE

## An Early History of Blackburn's Most Iconic Building

By Howard Foy and Chris Walton

Illustrated by Gosha Gibek

First published May 2024


ISBN: 978-1-7385500-0-5


Authors: Howard Foy & Chris Walton
Illustrations: Gosha Gibek

Re:Source Blackburn Press
King William Street, Blackburn, Lancashire BB1 7DT
info@exchangeblackburn.org.uk
www.exchangeblackburn.org.uk


Printed by Nu-Age Print & Copy
289 Padiham Road, Burnley, Lancashire. BB12 0HA


Designed by Gosh Art by Gosha Gibek
www.GoshaGibek.com

# CONTENTS

# ACKNOWLEDGEMENTS

National Lottery Heritage Fund. Kevin Penberthy, Mary Painter (Blackburn with Darwen Library and Information Service), Melanie Warren, Ray Smith (Blackburn Local History Society), Ian Holmes, Rob Wilkinson, Jack Bailey, Lord Charles Shuttleworth, The Rt Rev Philip North, Bishop of Blackburn, Rodrigo Guadarrama, https://www.cottontown.org (community history project), Hannah Beattie, Rebecca Johnson, (Blackburn Museum & Art Gallery), Lord Charles Shuttleworth, RIBA (Royal Institute of British Architects), Re:Ignite Church, Re:Source, Janet Burke, Anne Garlick, Lancashire Archives, Manchester Central Library, The National Archives.

# FOREWORDS

**The** renewal of a town or community requires two things. Pride in the past. Confidence in the future.

The town that forget its past or becomes ashamed of it loses its identity and risks becoming a pointless, joyless place.

The town that has no confidence in its future becomes lost in nostalgia and sadness for what once was.

That is why the renewal of The Exchange is such an important project for Blackburn. This extraordinary, neo-Gothic building looks back to the past because it holds so much of the story of Blackburn - its time as the powerhouse of the global cotton industry, its love for music, arts and entertainment and its religious debates.

And now, because of the bold plans of Re:Source, there is the opportunity for a renewed and regenerated Exchange to be a symbol of Blackburn's future. I am one of many who long for the day when once again this remarkable building can be fully restored as a place of gathering, of celebration and of worship.

This book tells a fascinating story of Blackburn's past. Let's hope it can inspire an even greater confidence in what the future holds.

*The Rt Revd Philip North,* *Bishop of Blackburn*

I know from my own experience as a chartered surveyor and property manager that the best way to look after great buildings is to use them. That is why I am so pleased, indeed excited, by the plans for The Exchange in the heart of Blackburn and delighted to have been invited to write a brief introduction to this history book.

The building was opened as the Cotton Exchange in 1865. Blackburn was then at the centre of Lancashire's textile industry, with mills all across the town. Even from the start, the building was used for a variety of purposes, and was the venue for many famous people, such as Charles Dickens, giving readings and talks for the public. As the textile trade went into decline at the end of the 19th century, The Exchange found new life and purpose, becoming a cinema in 1908.

That use continued for much of the 20th century, but the building itself deteriorated, and eventually large parts were in serious disrepair and unsuitable for public events.

When I first visited The Exchange, inside it was a sad reminder of past glories, though the superb architecture and façade was still evident. It now faces conservation, transformation and rebirth, and it will become a showcase venue for the whole community. It will be another example of the hope and determination for improvement for so much that is going on in Blackburn, following on from the development of the Cathedral Quarter.

I commend the business plans to all who want to play a part in Blackburn's regeneration story, in which The Exchange can be a shining symbol. I congratulate all those people and organisations who have brought together this story and everyone working hard to build the future of this fine building, I look forward to The Exchange being back in full use again soon.

*Lord Charles Shuttleworth*

# PREFACE

*'The Exchange' painting by Gosha Gibek, 2020*

**This** is the third local history book about an historic building in Blackburn that I have been privileged to coordinate as part of community engagement programmes supported by the National Lottery Heritage Fund; *James Dixon's Children* by Melanie Warren (2012) based on the records and diaries of Blackburn Orphanage (Child Action Northwest) and *The Fall and Rise of the Empire* by Melanie Warren (2010), based on the archives and oral histories of The Empire Cinema, now the Blackburn Empire theatre at Ewood, Blackburn.

However, this project has been a very different experience. To begin with, we were almost starting from scratch as there was no physical archive or written chronology that existed. So, from the start, our team of volunteer history detectives had a more difficult job, finding and piecing together newspaper articles, visiting collections, studying ephemera, researching and cross referencing a range of sources.

Sadly, Melanie Warren became ill before she could start work with us and died in 2023. We also lost Ray Smith, Blackburn Local History Society who had supported the previous publications with additional research and resources.

With no author and no archive, we weren't sure how we were going to tackle such an enormous task. Amazingly though, when we appealed for volunteers, we were blessed with the right people with the right skills at the right time. Howard Foy, a retired journalist with a passion for the town and the era, and Chris Walton, compelled by a deep curiosity to discover, preserve and share the hidden histories of this remarkable building. Together, Howard and Chris have quickly and quietly led this process with meticulous attention to detail and a humble desire to leave a lasting, professional and accurate legacy, so that others can finally access the history and understand the significance of this amazing place.

During the lockdown of 2020-2021, Gosha Gibek produced an amazing painting of The Exchange. It was a delight to be able to commission Gosha to illustrate the stories, and then a surprise to discover that her university degree and passion is book design. Wow, what a team!

We are also hugely grateful to librarian, Mary Painter from the Community History department at Blackburn Library who has taken an active interest in this project, supporting the staff and volunteer history detectives and introducing us to many helpful resources, local history enthusiasts and experts.

*Harriet Roberts*

It has been a pleasure working with all The Exchange staff and volunteers throughout this current project. I feel that Blackburn Central Library has benefitted from developing contacts and sharing information with this dedicated research group. Piecemeal evidence and scattered fragments of information have been gathered from many sources in order to reveal a more thorough and considered history of the Exchange which also reflects the social history of Blackburn during this period. This book has been long overdue, and it is an important contribution to the history of the town.

*Mary Painter*

*Blackburn with Darwen Library and Information Service*

# HOWARD FOY

*Photography by Rodrigo Guadarrama*

I'm Blackburn-born and bred, and after living and working in Manchester for more than 30 years, I returned to the area in 2015 following retirement as a production journalist on national newspapers. In a roundabout way, I heard that the Re:Source charity was looking for volunteers to help research the story of the Exchange as part of their exciting plan to bring the building back to life, and I knew at once that I wanted to be involved in the project.

I have been passionately interested in local history since I was a young schoolboy and my association with the Exchange dates back to that time as well. My first visits to the building were at the age of six or seven, when my father took me and my younger brother to the "Majestic" for haircuts at the barber's in the basement in King William Street.

I can also remember several visits to the Essoldo cinema, as it was called in the 1950s and 1960s. I cannot now recall any particular films from the early days, but I recently found an old diary which I kept as a teenager and I note that at the age of 17 in February 1968 - and therefore "under aged" - I sneaked into the Essoldo to see the X-rated film, Bonnie and Clyde.

It is not the building's days as a cinema that particularly interested me, however. The fact that it was commissioned by the mill-owners and textile merchants of Blackburn as the Cotton Exchange, a place where these eminent businessmen could congregate for commerce and relaxation, has always seemed fascinating - and it was both frustrating and surprising that very little existed in written form about its story.

When it opened in 1865, the Cotton Exchange highlighted my home town's proud position as one of the leading cotton weaving centres in Britain - if not the world - in the mid-Victorian era, and I wanted to help in finding out as much as I could about its genesis and history, both as a place of commerce and later as Blackburn's premier concert and assembly hall in the latter years of the 19th Century.

As things turned out, the bulk of the research for this book was carried out by my indefatigable colleague Chris Walton, who has spent many hours delving into archives both locally and nationally to diligently piece together the full story of the Exchange from the 1840s through to its sale and conversion to a cinema in 1920. But I have been pleased and honoured to be able to turn all his hard work into what I trust is a readable and entertaining narrative, encompassing not only the early history of the building itself but also touching on the development of Blackburn's major public edifices, including the Town Hall and Public Halls at Blakey Moor.

*Howard Foy*

# CHRIS WALTON

*Photography by Rodrigo Guadarrama*

**Growing** up in Darwen, I've many memories of visits to the Apollo 5 Cinema, watching classics like Toy Story and Jurassic Park, as well as the birthday parties downstairs at Tiggis Restaurant, complete with the birthday cake and music. In recent years, when Re:Source took over the building, I was curious about their plans to restore the Exchange and bring it back into use. When they called for volunteers, I signed up, keen to contribute in any way possible.

Initially, when I offered to research the history of the Exchange, I thought it would be a simple task of browsing through a few old books and newspapers.

However, it turned out to be a much deeper dive. Over the past year, I've delved into archives, sifted through newspapers, and even had the opportunity to handle artifacts at Blackburn Museum and Art Gallery. My journey has taken me from Preston to London in search of centuries-old forgotten documents.

Exploring the Exchange's past has been like solving a puzzle, with each discovery leading to another intriguing piece of the puzzle. It's been a fascinating journey that has deepened my appreciation for the history of our town and the role of the Exchange.

I'm grateful to Harriet Roberts, Caer Butler, and Lisa Clarke from Re:Source for their support and for welcoming me into the Exchange team. Special thanks also go to Mary Painter from Blackburn Central Library, Kevin Penberthy, and others who provided valuable resources and guidance, and to Howard Foy for writing up our research in to this book. Together, we've brought the Exchange out of obscurity, uncovering its rich history as a gathering place for traders, a venue for notable events, and a cherished part of our community. It's been an honour to be part of the effort to preserve and share its story.

*Chris Walton*

# GOSHA GIBEK

*Photography by Rodrigo Guadarrama*

In the bustling heart of Blackburn stands a majestic testament to history, the Cotton Exchange building. For me, this architectural marvel became more than just a subject for painting; it captured my imagination and ignited a passion for storytelling through art. When I was commissioned to paint a depiction of this iconic landmark, I knew it was a project close to my heart. My love for painting architecture, coupled with my signature use of vibrant colours, compelled me to showcase the building in all its splendour. Little did I know that this painting would pave the way for an exciting new chapter in my artistic journey.

As fate would have it, the opportunity to illustrate a book about the Cotton Exchange building presented itself, and I couldn't have been more thrilled. Drawing from my background in book design from the Academy of Fine Arts in Wroclaw, Poland, I eagerly embraced the chance to merge my passion for illustration with my expertise in layout and design. What began as a request for illustrations blossomed into a full-fledged collaboration, allowing me to infuse every page with creativity and artistry.

For me, book design is not just about embellishing text with images; it's about transforming words into visual masterpieces. From arranging text on the page to highlighting individual letters, every aspect of the design process excites me. And with my signature gloss painting technique, I aim to elevate the narrative further. By allowing the paint to drip freely on the paper, I create fluid and dynamic images reminiscent of cotton threads, echoing the essence of the Cotton Exchange building itself.

As you embark on this captivating journey through the history of the Exchange Building in Blackburn, I hope my illustrations transport you to a bygone era, where the echoes of its glory days resonate through the pages. Get ready to immerse yourself in the rich tapestry of stories and let my artwork guide you through the corridors of time.

*Gosha Gibek*

# NOTE

**Much** of the historical research for this book is taken from contemporary publications such as The Blackburn Times where we found the words, 'Exchange' and 'Cotton Exchange' were usually capitalised. These terms refer to the Blackburn Exchange which existed as an organised trading activity as early as the 1830s and had a number of meeting places before The Exchange as a physical building was built. Similarly, 'Town Hall' is a shortened reference to Blackburn Town Hall and is also capitalised. The terms News Room and Commercial Room are also usually capitalised in publications of the time and so, for consistency, these terms are also capitalised throughout this book.

# CHAPTER I
# COTTON TOWN

**Blackburn** and the surrounding communities of North-East Lancashire have been involved in the manufacture of cloth through the processes of spinning and weaving on a commercial scale since the days of the Tudors in the late 15th Century. Yarn spun from the wool of locally-reared sheep was turned into bales of cloth on hundreds of primitive handlooms powered by foot-treadles and operated by local folk in their own homes.

The finished product would then be purchased by merchants for onward sale to garment manufacturers in this country and abroad.

The weaving of cloth for personal use, using local raw materials, can be traced back many centuries, of course. If a family could produce enough textiles for their own purposes, then that was all that was required. One can only speculate on how and why these simple domestic arrangements developed in Blackburn during the reigns of Henry VII and his son Henry VIII into a commercial operation in which weaving families started producing a surplus and trading that for other goods, or selling it. By the mid-1500s, however, this cottage industry had developed to such an extent that a handful of local entrepreneurs set themselves up as merchants, buying in the surplus cloth from families and selling it on.

This trade had gained such importance that in 1566, Elizabeth I's ministers appointed a special Government officer to oversee the town's output. His duty was to inspect and measure any cloth intended for export, being on a careful lookout for faulty or sub-standard production. By this time, it is said that woollen cloth made in Blackburn was being sold to the Continent.

But it would be a switch from wool to cotton weaving in the early 1600s that really started Blackburn on the long road to becoming, by 1900, what one historian described as "the weaving capital of the world". Raw cotton was first imported to Britain from the West Indies and the new American colonies in the first years of the 17th Century, and as Liverpool was one of the main ports of entry, Blackburn's textile merchants presumably realised the potential profits to be made by switching from woollen to cotton cloth. It is said that the climate of North-East Lancashire is particularly suited to cotton spinning and weaving as the thread, which is finer than woollen thread, is less prone to breaking in the predominantly damp atmosphere.

Unlike with woollen cloth, where the basic raw material was available locally, handloom weavers had to acquire the cotton from merchants, sometimes referred to as undertakers, who purchased the raw bales as they were landed at Liverpool or elsewhere. The system was known as "Putting out". The merchants, many of them based in Manchester, employed delivery men, known as chapmen, who would tour Blackburn and surrounding towns with trains of pack-horses supplying cotton to the spinners at their homes, or to special communal buildings called "Putting out shops".

A quantity of raw cotton was weighed and given out to the operative, with a ticket showing the actual weight. The same weight, less a small percentage for wastage, had to be returned in cloth woven to a required pattern, and the merchant would then pay the weaver and arrange for the finishing of the cloth by specialist fullers and dyers, before its onward sale to garment manufacturers or at local markets.

To add strength in the early days, the cotton weft was increasingly combined with a linen warp to produce a fairly coarse product known as fustians. Flax-growing and drying to produce linen had been carried out in the Liverpool area since at least 1540 and linen production soon spread to other Lancashire towns. The result was a plain cotton-linen cloth for bleaching which became known as "Blackburn Greys", while the town also became well-known for a distinctive cloth with some of the warp threads and some of the weft being dyed blue to create a blue-and-white checked appearance, which gained the name "Blackburn Checks".

When Charles II came to the throne in 1660, Blackburn's population was estimated at just 1,160, and a register held that year listed 28 families in the town where the head of household was a "webster", an archaic word for a spinner or weaver. But as the Lancashire cotton trade developed, more and more families would take up spinning and weaving, either as their main source of income or to supplement earnings from other business activities, and the spinning wheel and handloom became essential items of household furniture in many homes.

Their influence on house design can be seen in old cottages that still exist in Blackburn and the surrounding area to this day, with long rows of windows, often going the full length of the building, to give as much light as possible for working the loom. Local carpenters and furniture makers were in demand to build handlooms and as the main components were standardised, they could be made very quickly.

By the 1720s, when Blackburn's population was believed to be still considerably less than 5,000, the growth in cotton weaving can be gauged by the fact that local parish registers record the names of 391 families so engaged. Marriage registers for the years 1704-07 show that almost 50% of the men tying the knot during that period declared their employment as weavers. In 1760, the celebrated traveller and writer the Rev Richard Pococke visited North-East Lancashire and described Blackburn in one of his journals as "a town which thrives by the cotton and woollen manufacture".

In fact, the town grew by an estimated 350% between 1600 and 1801, when the first official UK census recorded a population of 11,980, and it is said that the increase was almost entirely due to families abandoning a largely agrarian life on poor arable land in the neighbourhood to concentrate on spinning and weaving. The "Putting out" system controlled the business of cotton cloth manufacture in Blackburn for more than a century, but the 1720s also saw the first stirrings of the Industrial Revolution, which would dramatically transform the manufacturing processes of the cotton trade over the next century-and-a-half.

Several ground-breaking inventions in textile machinery occurred in a relatively short time during the middle years of the 18th Century. In 1733, John Kay of Bury invented the Flying Shuttle which enabled weavers to weave faster. In 1764, James Hargreaves, a handloom weaver who was born in the hamlet of Stanhill, near Oswaldtwistle, invented the Spinning Jenny, the first machine which could spin thread quicker and more efficiently than a traditional spinning wheel - producing up to 20 spools of yarn in the same time that a hand-operated wheel could produce one.

Then in 1779, Samuel Crompton of Bolton produced his Spinning Mule, which once again dramatically increased the amount of cotton that could be spun at any one time. Instead of having workers creating spindles of cotton thread one at a time, one operator could now use the machine to spin hundreds of spindles at once. The 1770s also saw Preston-born Richard Arkwright patenting his Water Frame, a spinning machine powered by a water-wheel, which was first set to work in a new factory in Cromford, Derbyshire.

The first water-powered spinning mills in Lancashire quickly followed. In 1777, Arkwright was employed by local entrepreneur Edward Chadwick to set up a mill on the banks of the River Yarrow at Birkacre, near Chorley, while W.A. Abram, in his 1877 History of Blackburn, records the first water-powered cotton-spinning mill in Blackburn being opened in about 1775 in Wensley Fold, with a second mill being established at Mill Hill around 1790.

Increasingly, the merchants acquiring supplies of raw cotton from the ports now went into business as cotton spinners themselves in purpose-built mills, or made way for other entrepreneurs to take over the trade. The mechanisation of the spinning process meant the days of the domestic spinning wheel were numbered, but this allowed the cotton operatives to concentrate on weaving the cloth on their handlooms, receiving spun yarn from the mills as their basic material instead of raw cotton.

However, water power would soon be eclipsed by a more efficient way to mechanise the cloth-making process - steam power. Blackburn was well-placed to profit from the new processes as it was situated on the North-East Lancashire coalfield, with abundant fuel supplies at hand. Water power was much cheaper than coal as long as supplies were not affected by the weather - freezing in winter and drying up in summer - but once the power loom was introduced, coal was needed to fire the boilers and create the steam to set banks of semi-automatic looms in motion.

The first power looms were built in the Midlands around 1790, but they were primitive affairs, and it took more than two decades of development before Lancashire's mill owners would start to trust in the new technology. Blackburn's first two steam-powered mills were built on the banks of the River Blakewater, but when the Leeds-Liverpool Canal was completed in 1818, a major expansion of Blackburn's mechanised textile industry got under way with six new and bigger steam-powered mills being built alongside the canal in the 1820s. The new waterway offered not only a ready mode of transport for both coal and cotton, but also a secure source of water for the boilers.

Several more large combined spinning and weaving mills opened in the town during the 1830s, but the following decade also saw the introduction of a number of separate weaving businesses operating from large purpose-built steam-powered weaving sheds. This bolstered Blackburn's reputation as an emerging centre of Lancashire's power-loom weaving trade.

Incidentally, the development of the steam-powered loom did not kill off the handloom, as may have been thought. In 1802, William Ratcliffe of Stockport patented a new type of handloom with an iron frame and mechanical improvements which was said to boost productivity for the average handloom weaver by around 50%. It was known as the Dandy Loom, and several were installed in mills in Blackburn or in smaller premises known as "Dandy loom shops".

One site where they were installed was the Jubilee Mill on the corner of Jubilee Street and what became the Boulevard in the centre of the town (later the site of the Palace Cinema). The narrow thoroughfare that ran past this mill and which still links the Boulevard with Darwen Street and the Cathedral gardens preserves the memory of centuries of handloom weaving in the town in its name, Dandy Walk.

## CHAPTER 2
# AT THE OLD BULL

**By** the 1840s, the factory system was completely established, the power loom was king, and there were 35 cotton mills in Blackburn operating a total of 150,000 spindles and 12,000 looms. By 1860, the number of mills had increased to 78, with one million spindles and 29,000 looms, while no less than 29 new spinning or weaving mills were being planned or under construction in the town and surrounding area.

It was calculated that by that time the spinning mills of Blackburn were consuming 4,000 bales of cotton worth £50,000 each week, producing one million pounds in weight of yarn for weaving, and the annual value of the woven cloth which resulted was around £9million. The mill owners had to find buyers for all this output. In 1809, Manchester's Royal Exchange opened as a focal point for Lancashire's cotton manufacturers from the likes of Preston, Bolton, Bury, Rochdale and Oldham, as well as Blackburn, to congregate to buy and sell spun yarn and woven fabrics.

However, Blackburn soon developed its own "exchange" in the form of the Old Bull Inn, which stood for many years facing the old Market Place at the corner of what is now Church Street and Darwen Street. An accounts book held in Blackburn Library records a first formal gathering of an Exchange and Newsroom in 1834, when a meeting was held to set their rules of operation and to list the members. It is not known exactly when the cotton merchants and traders first met at the Old Bull, but historian W.A. Abram, writing in the Blackburn Standard in 1890, explained that the public house "served as a commercial meeting-place or Exchange for the town".

Part of the pub was reserved for a Commercial Room, open only to subscribers, where the town's traders and manufacturers - not just in the cotton business - could get together. According to Abram, every Wednesday afternoon between 3pm and 5pm, Manchester yarn agents and prominent Blackburn cotton spinners and manufacturers would "stand on the flags in front of the entrance to the inn discussing the markets, and giving and taking orders for yarns".

The Old Bull, which was previously known as the Black Bull, had been in existence as a public house for at least 150 years - and possibly more than 200. In fact, historian George Miller, in his 1970 book Blackburn's Old Inns, says there was a hostelry on this site for at least 500 years. Yet it wasn't, apparently, the first place in Blackburn to perform this trading function. In another 1890 article in the Blackburn Standard, possibly also written by Abram, mention was made of proposed building alterations then being considered in the Northgate area of the town. The writer pointed out that this was "a historic portion" which had been for many years a regular meeting place for townsfolk.

He wrote: "Across the way was a broad footpath known as the Cotton Exchange, and it was here that the local cotton manufacturers responsible for the handloom industry would meet to buy and sell, and to discuss the topics of the day. In the off-streets like Cannon Street, Queen Street and Duke Street were warehouses where these manufacturers received the woven cloth from the handloom weavers and put out their yarn for next week's operations."

The first mention of erecting a building to house the Cotton Exchange has been traced back to 1819, when Joseph Feilden, the Lord of the Manor of Blackburn - who owned almost half of the land in the town - reportedly offered open space adjoining the Tacketts Fields for construction of a Town Hall and Exchange. The Tacketts Fields, three in number, were located to the north of the built-up part of the town centre, roughly in the area where Richmond Terrace, Tontine Street and Barbara Castle Way can now be found, and the land in question is presumed to be where the Town Hall, or Library and Museum were later built. Although nothing came of the offer, Feilden had presumably calculated that the growing town must inevitably expand in that direction, and, in fact, developers soon moved into the area to build the fine Georgian parade of Richmond Terrace.

Returning to the 1840s, the Old Bull "Exchange" was clearly as important to the businessmen and traders in Blackburn as the Royal Exchange was to the manufacturers in Manchester, and with the volume of trade increasing month by month, it was increasingly desirable that Blackburn, too, should have a dedicated building in which this commerce could take place. According to the Blackburn Standard, "the want of an Exchange has long been the topic of conversation especially since the Blackburn commercials market has assumed the importance which has characterised it within the last ten years".

In 1845, a committee was formed of several of the most important merchants and manufacturers in the town and neighbourhood, including William Henry Hornby, first Mayor of Blackburn, MP for the town and later national leader of the Conservative Party, Sir William Feilden, 1st Baronet of Feniscowles, the son of Joseph Feilden, and also formerly the town's MP, and Eccles Shorrock, the man who commissioned the building of Darwen's India Mill with its massive Venetian-style chimney which still stands over the town.

They purchased a plot of land opposite the Old Bull Inn on which stood a couple of shops overlooking the old Market Place - the current site of

Lloyds Bank - and adjacent to another pub, the New Bull, which opened into Fleming Square. A competition was launched inviting "architects, builders and others" to submit plans for a suitable building, and an advertisement in the Blackburn Standard of 3rd February stated: "A bonus of £50 will be given for the best approved Plan, with Elevations and Sections, of a PUBLIC EXCHANGE, intended to be erected in the Market Place in the Town of Blackburn." Further prizes of £20 and £10 respectively were on offer for the plans deemed to be second and third.

In due course, thirty entries were displayed at the Assembly Room in Heaton Street, and the celebrated architect Charles Robert Cockerell, designer of the National Monument of Scotland in Edinburgh and St George's Hall in Liverpool, was invited to judge the submitted designs. The competition coincided with separate plans by the town's Improvement Commissioners - precursors of the borough council - to knock down much of the Old Bull and rebuild it further back from the street to permit a wider foot-pavement of at least seven feet and to remove overhanging gables from the upper storeys. It was also intended to modernise the interior so as to provide for "the needs of a first-class house in a great town like Blackburn was growing into".

Ten of the 30 competition submissions for the new Cotton Exchange were forwarded to Professor Cockerell for his final judgement, and amongst the stipulations of the committee was that the frontage of the building facing the old Market Square should incorporate a well-lit News Room - said to be the most important feature - where newspapers and other periodicals would be available for members to read. Apparently it was also suggested that the New Bull Inn should be incorporated into the general plan. This, said the committee, would "add to the dignity of the building as well as to the repute of the Inn itself".

It was further stated that Professor Cockerell and the 10 architects who had submitted final designs for consideration were in agreement that a tower should be a characteristic feature and the style should be "Grecian or Italian in preference to Gothic or any other style". The winning entry by William Hayward Brakspear and Thomas Dickson of Manchester was in the Classical Revival style. Front and side elevations of their proposed design can be viewed on the Royal Institute of British Architects (RIBA) website.

Unfortunately, with Britain suddenly plunging into a recession at that time, the building plans were put on hold for a couple of years before it was announced that the project was back under way in November 1849. This news was warmly welcomed by the Blackburn Standard, with a report that fund-raising for the building would start in the new year, and the newspaper stated: "We confidently anticipate that the time is not far distant when the commercial interests of Blackburn will have reason to congratulate themselves on the possession of an edifice which will at once prove an ornament to the town and an honour to its mercantile enterprise."

In early 1850, adverts were duly placed in the local press and it was announced that the committee was seeking to raise £20,000 to fund the building by inviting members of the public to buy shares of £10 each. In case any townsfolk questioned the need for a permanent Cotton Exchange building, the Blackburn Standard, in a further article on the revived plans, stated boldly: "The thriving and populous town of Blackburn - the seat of many of the most important original inventions and modern improvements connected with the textile manufactures of the county, and the centre of trading operations carried out in the most enterprising manner and on a scale of magnitude only exceeded by Manchester - has long felt the need of a suitable public erection, presenting adequate accommodation for the great number of merchants, manufacturers and other commercial gentlemen frequenting its market, and offering the requisite facilities for the transaction of the extensive business for which this locality has been so long distinguished."

In June of the following year, a progress report on the fund-raising revealed that the appeal had attracted a large number of small contributors to add to the £500 each already subscribed by the eight well-to-do members of the committee. But sadly, with only around half of the £20,000 needed for the project having been raised by February 1851, the committee reluctantly decided to cancel the scheme, and the site they had purchased was put up for auction. In the meantime, the rebuilding of the Old Bull across the old Market Place had been completed, with a new Commercial Room, and it resumed its role as an unofficial Cotton Exchange for the merchants and manufacturers to hold their weekly get-togethers.

One such meeting on 23rd November, 1853, made headlines in national newspapers, and was even mentioned in the House of Commons, when it was the scene of what the press described as a "riot" by cotton workers in the town. The reason for the disturbance is somewhat confusing. Cotton workers in nearby Preston were striking for better wages, although the dispute had not affected the mills in Blackburn and surrounding areas. However, there was an apparent false rumour in the town that the Preston mill owners attending the meeting that afternoon would be appealing to the Blackburn manufacturers to shut their own mills temporarily, thereby preventing Blackburn workers from sending some of their wages to their Preston comrades to help them prolong the strike.

Consequently, it appears that the Preston mill owners present were forcibly ejected from the public house and driven from the town. It is said that serious violence was only avoided by letting six members of the mob search the pub room-by-room to ensure all members of the Preston contingent were rounded up. Apparently, Blackburn could only muster 10 constables at the time who proved powerless to intervene, and no arrests were made. The incident was undoubtedly alarming to the town's senior cotton manufacturers and merchants, but in fact the Old Bull's days as their regular meeting place were now numbered.

In 1851, Blackburn gained municipal borough status, with the right to elect its own town council, and many of those senior businessmen were elected to the council, or supported others who won seats. In October 1856, the new Town Hall opened, and on 1st January, 1857, an Exchange and News Room was established by the council on the south side of the building's entrance vestibule, open to "parties residing, or having places of business within the borough" at an annual subscription of £1 and 5 shillings.

At the same time, the subscribers to the Commercial Room at the Old Bull voted unanimously to vacate the pub and take up the council's offer of the new premises, with the cotton merchants and traders resuming their weekly Exchange activities in the Town Hall's vestibule and on the front steps from 7th January. It was the end of an era for the Old Bull, but not the end of the establishment's role as a watering hole and meeting place at the heart of the town. The pub finally closed and was demolished in 1950 - still proudly bearing the name Old Bull Inn over the front door.

# CHAPTER 3
# SUUM CUIQUE

**While** it was generally agreed that the new Exchange facilities at the Town Hall were an improvement on the accommodation which had been provided at the Old Bull, it was only a matter of a few days into 1858 before some of the leading businessmen in the town began talking again about the possibility of building a meeting place of their own. As the Blackburn Standard reported on 21st January, the old Market Place site remained unsold and was still held by trustees appointed by the original organising committee - and the plans for the building were still available. It was suggested that a new committee would be formed very shortly to revive the project.

In due course, a sub-committee of the subscribers was put together to consider the idea, but there was apparently no further progress until almost two years later when the entire membership of the Town Hall Exchange met for their annual meeting on the 29th November, 1859. By this time, the sub-committee had drawn up a report in which it was stated that as the Exchange membership was now in excess of 400, the Town Hall room was no longer big enough for their needs. It was also pointed out that it was likely that the room would, in any case, soon be required by the council for other purposes.

While there was no mention of reviving the original Cotton Exchange project, the sub-committee suggested that a new meeting place was now needed, and one "suitable in every respect" could be built for £5,000. It was further suggested that funds could be raised by selling 1,200 shares at £5 each. However, several members felt that more than a new meeting room was needed and pressed for a revival of the project to build a more substantial Exchange with associated Commercial and News Rooms which had been cancelled in 1851.

The momentum was now growing, and within a fortnight another meeting was called on Wednesday, 14th December, to discuss the matter further. The Blackburn Standard reported that the room was crowded, but as the hum of the normal day's business was still going forward, few of those present could see or hear what was being debated. Nevertheless, it became clear that there was now strong support for a return to the 1851 scheme, and a provisional committee was appointed to look into possible sites for a building.

The subscribers re-convened at the Town Hall a month later on 11th January, 1860, with the Mayor, Councillor James Cunningham in the chair, although the gathering was called at short notice and only about 20 of the 400-plus members were in attendance apart from the provisional committee. The Mayor reported that four possible sites had been inspected and were under consideration.

First was the original site in the old Market Place opposite the Old Bull Inn, but it was suggested that this would be too expensive to re-develop now, possibly because they could no longer incorporate the New Bull into their plans as originally intended. The committee also looked at a plot of land of 1,766 square yards on the corner of Ainsworth Street and

Victoria Street and at a neighbouring site of 1,342 square yards next to the Police Court and adjacent to the new Market Place at the rear of the Town Hall.

The fourth site was almost directly opposite the front of the Town Hall, including the recently-erected Feilden's Arms public house, on the corner of King William Street and Town Hall Street (previously known as Thunder Alley). At 2,286 square yards, it was the largest of the four sites, and though the cost of purchase had been estimated at £2 6s per square yard, it was cheaper than the smaller Ainsworth Street plot, which was calculated at £2 12s 4d per square yard.

One possible problem was that the Catholic Brethren had already taken possession of part of the plot on Town Hall Street and had laid out the foundations for a new Catholic Hall. Nevertheless, the Mayor said the committee felt that the Feilden's Arms site was the "most eligible", with Ainsworth Street being the next best, and he proposed that they should look further into acquiring one or the other without delay. Committee member Thomas Lund, in seconding the proposal, explained to the gathering that he had already been deputed with other committee members to meet representatives of the Catholic Brethren to see if they would consider giving up the site.

The response had been favourable, with the Brethren indicating to him that "not in the slightest manner would they stand in the way of any public good" - although they would, of course, want compensation for the small outlay that had already been expended on laying out the foundations of their hall. Mr Lund then went on to say that the preferred site would be more convenient than Ainsworth Street for the townsmen who used the Exchange as a News Room, as there was enough space to have a News Room which could be quite separate to the main area of the Exchange.

One of the members asked if the new public house, which had only opened in 1855, would have to be pulled down, and Alderman William Stones replied that it would, but he said it was "seldom they could get a piece of land with such a commanding frontage at such a price". He added that it was proposed that the full frontage would not be dedicated to the Exchange, but there would be space for eight or nine shops which would bring in a considerable revenue, and they intended to retain the public house licence so that one of the proposed shops could perhaps be licensed as a refreshment room for visitors to the adjacent News Room.

Alderman Stones also said that in purchasing the full site, which included two adjacent plots of land at the rear, they would still have sufficient space to permit the Catholic Brethren to build a new hall for themselves further along Town Hall Street. After some further discussion on whether the manufacturers and ordinary people of Blackburn would support the plans, it was unanimously resolved that a new Exchange should be built for the town at a proposed cost of £12,000, the money to be raised by selling £10 shares.

A new committee was appointed, made up of the Mayor, the borough's two MPs, William Henry Hornby and James Pilkington, and many of the principal resident merchants and manufacturers, and it was also agreed that a company be formed to take the project forward. Advertisements were then placed in local newspapers containing a form of application for shares and including a full list of the 24 members of the committee, which amounted to a rollcall of the great and the good of the town and the surrounding area, namely:

James Cunningham, Mayor
William Henry Hornby MP
James Pilkington MP
John Baynes
William Dudley Coddington
William Dickinson
J B Deakin
Thomas Dugdale
Joseph Eccles
Thomas Eccles (Lower Darwen)
Thomas Eccles (Wensley Fold)
John Fish
William Harrison
Robert Hopwood
R Raynsford Jackson
John Livesey
Thomas Lund
David Nicol
Eccles Shorrock
John Sparrow
William Stones
George Walmsley
Nathaniel Walsh
Robert Watson

The adverts were placed in the name of the Blackburn Exchange Company Ltd, which had been formally registered to oversee the building project. This was a successor to the Blackburn Exchange Building Company, which had been registered on the 20th April, 1850, for the original scheme. It is believed that this company was later dissolved or re-registered under the new name in 1860. Thirteen members of the committee were appointed as directors of the company, including James Cunningham, who became the chairman, while solicitor Thomas Crook Ainsworth also joined the board as company secretary.

As thoughts were turning to the possible layout of the proposed building, there was a surprising new development in early Spring which could have had marked consequences for the final scheme. Post Office officials had just declared that Blackburn's existing post office on King Street was now totally inadequate for the needs of the growing borough, and on 11th April, a Post Office assistant surveyor attended a meeting of the Exchange committee when it was agreed that they would look into the possibility of including a new post office and telegraph office in their plans. Such a move would no doubt boost the profitability of the development as well as being a boon to businessmen using the Exchange.

The final details of the proposed scheme were then published in May 1860. There was to be an Exchange Hall on the ground floor covering 800 square yards which could be adapted as an assembly or concert room, a News or Reading Room alongside of 100 square yards, plus a post office and telegraph office, office accommodation, a spacious vestibule and basement space for offices or warehouses. It was also suggested that provision should be made for a possible extension of the Exchange Hall to run further along King William Street towards Sudell Cross. At the front of the property, it was proposed that there would be eight or nine shops from which they could expect a substantial revenue, with the Exchange Hall immediately behind them.

At the first annual meeting of the company, on 1st May, 1860, it was revealed that 571 shares had been taken up to create an operating capital of £5,710. It was now confirmed that the committee had settled on the proposed site facing the Town Hall, adjoining and including the three-storey Feilden's Arms, and the public house was being purchased for the purpose. A month earlier, on 4th April, advertisements had again been placed in the local press inviting architects and builders to submit plans, specifications and estimates for "a building to contain a large room for Exchange purposes, a News Room, Committee and other rooms for the transaction of business" with cash prizes for the best three submissions.

Presumably due to the late addition of a post office and telegraph office to the original plans, the deadline for submissions was extended by two months to 1st August, but just nine days later it was announced that William Hayward Brakspear, who had been joint winner of the competition for the Market Place site, had again submitted the best proposal, pocketing another

£50 prize in the process. His winning design, which was curiously named Suum Cuique (classical Latin for "Each to his own" or "May all get their due"), was described in the Blackburn Standard as being in the "English Pointed" style associated with the 15th Century - more commonly known as Victorian Gothic.

To match the site's frontage, which was angled to follow the curve of King William Street towards Sudell Cross, it featured a central tower with matching wings on either side. The main Exchange room, which at 800 square yards was four times the size of the Town Hall meeting room, was to be in the right-hand wing, while the News Room and supporting rooms would be in the left-hand wing. The estimated building cost would be £6,000, with the architect being paid a commission of 5%, with several thousand pounds extra to be spent on interior decoration, fixtures and fittings.

No doubt to assure readers that Brakspear was the right man for the job, the newspaper went on to point out that he had learned his craft as a pupil of Sir Charles Barry, the architect responsible for rebuilding the Houses of Parliament in the 1840s after a major fire. Construction was set to begin before the end of 1861, and, indeed, tenders for the building work had already been advertised earlier in the year.

Bids were slow in coming in, however, mainly due to a series of strikes in the trade, and when tenders were eventually received from several building firms, the company considered them to be so far in excess of the architect's estimates that they rejected them all. However they felt it was important to get the project under way, and it was decided to employ two local builders, Richard Hacking and Henry Sellers, to prepare the preliminary excavations and put in the foundations and lay out the cellars up to basement level.

In the meantime, it appears that the Catholic Brethren's apparent willingness to give up the site of their new hall in Town Hall Street had hit a stumbling block over the terms of the deal. The Brethren had asked for a payment of almost £1,600, but the company considered this to be excessive. The Exchange committee suggested the quoted figure would be the market value of the completed hall, but as work on the project had only recently started, they would be happy to re-imburse the Brethren for the money already spent with contractors, plus the original purchase price of the land, and an additional £250 by way of compensation for the inconvenience of having to find another site for their new meeting place.

The Brethren rejected this offer, and negotiations quickly reached a stalemate with directors of the Exchange Company suggesting that if there was no agreement they would go ahead with their building by adapting the plans to exclude the Town Hall Street plot. The deadlock generated comment in the local press, with some observers suggesting that the Brethren were perhaps being "exorbitant or unreasonable" in their demands, and the two committees should get together to work out an acceptable compromise.

The criticism prompted the Catholic Hall committee's secretary, Robert Davenport, to write to the Blackburn Times on 28th April to refute the accusations by laying out the various sums of money they had already spent and how much more they would need to find a new site for their project. Mr Davenport suggested the quoted figure of £1,588 18s 9d was a reasonable amount of recompense, particularly as the Exchange Company themselves agreed that by taking over the site, the value of the land would increase by £656 5s.

He went on: "Let the Exchange committee bear in mind that we know when we have a good situation, and also we know how far twenty shillings will pay, as well as they do. We are all working men, and have to toil hard for what we have, and it must not be supposed that we shall throw anything away to injure ourselves and benefit those who can better afford to lose a pound than a shilling."

As a result, the Brethren decided to continue with construction of their hall, and the Exchange committee reluctantly conceded that there would no longer be sufficient space for a parade of shops fronting King William Street, leading to a major revision of the plans, although an unintended consequence of this change would undoubtedly improve the architectural appearance of the completed building.

The Catholic Hall was duly completed in July 1860, when a flag was hoisted on the roof to mark the occasion. The building consisted of three large shops on the ground floor with a large assembly room above. However, for some reason it must have turned out to be unsatisfactory - or the Brethren simply had a change of heart - as the property was put up for auction just over three years later in October 1863. It was purchased by a property agent on behalf of the Exchange Company for £1,300 - although it later transpired that the company had not paid the full price but had actually taken out a mortgage, to be repaid later.

After the work on the Exchange foundations was completed, there was another delay until September 1862 while the company again sought tenders for the main construction work, and when some considerably reduced tenders were submitted, they agreed to employ Patrick Farrell, of Manchester, to complete the building for the sum of £7,935. At this point, a new cloud hung over the plans with Blackburn feeling the full effects of what became known as the Lancashire Cotton Famine.

Cotton mills in the town were struggling to keep the spinning machines and power looms working due to a shortage of raw materials following the outbreak of the American Civil War, as it was the slave-owning Southern states of the US which produced most of the world's raw cotton. But manufacturers had already begun reducing production due to a fall in demand for their cloth. The Lancashire cotton industry had just enjoyed two boom years in 1859 and 1860 when they produced more woven cotton than could be sold worldwide, making cutbacks inevitable. Across the county, thousands of mill workers lost their jobs as a result and local relief committees were set up to appeal for financial help for impoverished families.

Nevertheless, the Exchange Company continued to drive their plans forward, no doubt hoping that the disruption would only be temporary. In June 1862, a meeting of Blackburn's town council was discussing ways to help the poor of the borough when it was suggested that a sum of £1,000 that had been accrued in surplus subscriptions by the Town Hall Exchange committee should be paid to the town's relief fund. Members of the committee in attendance at the meeting objected, saying the money in all probability would be needed to aid the erection of the new Exchange, and the suggestion was quietly dropped.

On 29th November, 1862, the Preston Chronicle published two contrasting brief items in a round-up of news from neighbouring Blackburn. It was reported that a new soup kitchen had opened for out-of-work employees in Yates's Mill at Eanam, while just across the town centre, preliminary building work had now commenced on the new Exchange, with a forecast that construction would take 18 months to complete.

# CHAPTER 4
# A RED-LETTER DAY

**Barely** three months into the construction work, Tuesday, 10th March, 1863, was chosen as the day for a grand celebration to mark the laying of the new building's Foundation or Corner Stone. It was conceived as a double celebration, as that day was also the occasion of the marriage of Queen Victoria's son, Albert Edward, Prince of Wales, to Princess Alexandra of Denmark. A public holiday had been declared, and despite the fact that the event took place during a period of economic downturn, in the midst of the Cotton Famine, when many ordinary townsfolk were struggling with poverty, a lavish ceremony and day-long festivities were organised.

Under the circumstances, the directors of the Exchange Company expressed a hope that a grand day of celebration would both bring some much-needed cheer to the town and point the way towards a future prosperity in which the Cotton Exchange would have a central role. Ahead of the event, there had been fears that the day could be a washout as the previous Sunday had been wet and stormy and Monday was dark and gloomy. But fortunately it stayed fine and bright, if a little frosty. The Town Hall Square and the construction site of the new Exchange were decorated with flags and banners, with viewing platforms on which could sit the town's dignitaries, including businessmen, landowners and politicians, to witness the stone-laying.

The day began with 200 Artillery Volunteers marching to the Battery at the top of the recently-opened Corporation Park at Revidge to fire a Royal Salute. Marching back to the Town Hall, they were joined by about 250 Rifle Volunteers, and at 11am the two companies formed up at the head of a grand procession consisting of the Mayor and councillors, council officials, magistrates, clergy, directors and shareholders of the Exchange, merchants, tradesmen, and members of friendly societies including the Independent Order of Oddfellows and the Loyal Orangemen.

Watched and accompanied by throngs of townspeople, the procession started from the front of the Town Hall by way of Richmond Terrace, Preston New Road and East Park Road to the top (east) gate of Corporation Park. Moving into the park and on to the broad avenue near the largest of the two lakes, they then assembled on the sloping ground to watch as two oak trees, appropriately named Albert and Alexandra, were planted in honour of the Royal couple on either side of the avenue by the Lord of the Manor, Joseph Feilden, and Mrs Feilden.

The procession then formed up again and proceeded to exit the park on the west side and moved on via West Park Road, Montague Street, King Street, Back Lane, Darwen Street, Church Street, Victoria Street and across the new Market Place to the front of the Exchange on King William Street, arriving at about 12.30pm - coincidentally the time that the Royal wedding was getting under way in St George's Chapel at Windsor Castle.

There were loud cheers as Alderman William Harrison, a senior director of the Blackburn Exchange Company, then stepped forward to formally welcome the Mayor, Councillor James Sturdy, and to thank him for accepting the invitation to lay the Corner Stone. Alderman Harrison said: "It is highly appropriate that a building which marks the commercial progress and importance of the borough, which is designed to promote its prosperity, and which will certainly add to its architectural beauties, should be inaugurated by such a ceremony as this." He then handed the Mayor an engraved silver trowel containing the inscription:

PRESENTED TO HIS WORSHIP

JAMES BARLOW STEWARDSON STURDY, Esq,

Mayor of the Borough of Blackburn,

by the Directors of the BLACKBURN EXCHANGE CO.,

On his laying the Corner Stone

of the EXCHANGE BUILDINGS

ON THE 10th DAY OF MARCH, 1863

HRH ALBERT EDWARD, PRINCE OF WALES

AND HRH THE PRINCESS ALEXANDRA OF DENMARK

in the 26th Year OF THE REIGN

OF HER MAJESTY QUEEN VICTORIA

The Secretary of the Blackburn Exchange Company, Thomas Crook Ainsworth, then came forward with a large bottle containing coins of the realm, local newspapers and other documents as a "time capsule", which was placed in a cavity in the stone which had been specially prepared for it. He then read out aloud to the assembled company the words on a metal plaque which was to be affixed to the front of the stone, covering the cavity:

THE CORNER STONE OF THESE EXCHANGE

BUILDINGS was laid on the celebration of the wedding

of H.R.H. ALBERT EDWARD, PRINCE OF WALES AND

H.R.H. PRINCESS ALEXANDRA OF DENMARK,

ON THE 10TH DAY OF MARCH, 1863,

in the 26th Year of the Reign

of Her Majesty QUEEN VICTORIA,

BY JAMES BARLOW STEWARDSON STURDY, ESQ.,

Mayor of Blackburn.

DIRECTORS: James Cunningham, Chairman, John Baynes, Abraham Haworth, Joseph Harrison. John Sparrow, Eccles Shorrock, George Walmsley, Nathaniel Walsh, Robert Watson, Thomas Lund, David Nichol, James Dickinson, Wm, Dudley Coddington, and William Stones.

SECRETARY: Thomas Crook Ainsworth.

ARCHITECT: William Hayward Brakspear.

BUILDER: Patrick Farrell, William Henry Hornby M.p.

James Pilkington M.p.

GOD SAVE THE QUEEN.

Depositing the plate over the cavity, he said, to more loud cheers: "May the superstructure flourish." The stone was then spread with lime mortar and the Mayor gave a finishing touch with the trowel as the immense block was gently lowered by workmen into its intended resting place. Apparently, at this very moment, the clock on the new Market Hall nearby struck one, and a flag on the roof of the Town Hall was run up the mast to signify that the laying of the stone was complete.

There then followed some long and wordy speeches, with Alderman William Stones gifting the ceremonial trowel and an accompanying mallet on behalf of the Exchange Company to the Mayor, and expressing his hope that the new Exchange would "witness the return and increase of our commercial and industrial prosperity".

He added: "We all hope that the gloom which overhangs the present, and the cloud that obscures the future, will soon uplift and roll away, that Blackburn will soon again experience a renewal of the trade which, coupled with the energy of its inhabitants, has earned for it the character of one of the most enterprising and prosperous of the boroughs of Lancashire, and on the return of these better times will be better understood than at present the importance of the Exchange Building we are now assembled to inaugurate." Councillor Sturdy replied with effusive thanks before stepping forward once more to gently tap the stone with the mallet, saying, to more loud cheers: "I declare this stone now well and truly laid."

The Mayor then went on to speak of the major progress that had been made in Blackburn in the past 15 years, during which borough status had been granted to the town. He praised the Market Hall in King William Street, which had opened in 1848, the Town Hall next to it, the laying out and landscaping of Corporation Park, which opened in 1857, and the establishment, for the use of both the borough and the surrounding area, of an Infirmary.

The population of the town had grown from 36,629 at the 1841 census to 46,536 in 1851 and 63,125 in 1861, and he went on to say that the booming manufacturing and commercial business of the town had made a "distinct commodious building" to carry out that commerce a necessity. He said the new Exchange buildings would satisfy these requirements, as well as being readily adaptable for other purposes, and would be "a thing of beauty to everyone who sees it". Councillor Sturdy then thanked the directors of the Exchange Company for arranging the daylong celebrations and he added:

"I hope this day will long be remembered in Blackburn as a day of happiness and pleasure and rejoicing, and it will be a red-letter day in the calendar of the borough".

To loud and continuous cheering, the Rifle Volunteers then fired a salute and the assembled band played the National Anthem before the Mayor climbed up on the Corner Stone and called for three cheers for the Queen, the Prince of Wales and his new bride. More cheers followed before the ceremony was concluded with another salute fired by the Rifle Volunteers, after which a meal was laid on at the Town Hall for pensioners, old women resident at Turner's Almshouses at Whalley Banks and poor inmates of the borough's workhouses.

In the afternoon, two bands entertained revellers outside the Town Hall, and in the evening, a display of coloured lanterns illuminated the Town Hall Square before a huge bonfire was lit near the top of Corporation Park accompanied by fireworks on the Battery, with thousands of townsfolk converging on the park to enjoy the spectacle.

It appears, however, that not everyone in the town was impressed by the festivities. In a letter to the Blackburn Times a few days later, a correspondent using the pseudonym "Uncle Jonathan" suggested that the celebrations were weak and the public less than enthusiastic. Another correspondent questioned why the stone-laying ceremony had been performed by the Mayor, Alderman Sturdy, when it had previously been understood that the former Mayor, Alderman James Cunningham, would perform the task. He commented sarcastically: "By a little scheming, the worthy alderman is put to one side, and the new Mayor and new shareholder is to do the honours of the day."

In a postscript to the day's celebrations, it is perhaps understandable that the Exchange Company would seek to record the events for posterity, and Vladimir Ossipovitch Sherwood (1832-1897), a Russian-born artist, was chosen to create a painting of the stone-laying ceremony. He was the grandson of William Sherwood, an engineer who had moved to Moscow from England in 1800 at the invitation of Tsar Paul I to help develop the Russian cotton industry.

The artist had come to Blackburn in 1860 at the invitation of John Charles Dickinson, son of Exchange Company director James Dickinson, to paint portraits of its wealthy families. The two men had met in Russia when Dickinson was supplying looms made by his father's Blackburn foundry to cotton mills there. Sherwood stayed in Blackburn for about five years before returning to Russia, where he went on to have a notable career as a sculptor and an architect as well as a painter. He was responsible for the design of the State Historical Museum which stands proudly in Moscow's Red Square.

On the day of the stone-laying ceremony, he sketched the proceedings from a position high up on scaffolding which had been erected to lay the bricks of the back wall of the new building. This gave him a vantage point from the front of the Foundation Stone with the dignitaries surrounding it, overlooked by ladies on the platform that had been specially erected for them, with a view of the Town Hall and the assembled throng at the rear. In creating his painting, the main players in the ceremony all sat later for separate portraits to be included in the composition, and in a progress report on the work in mid-April an appeal was issued for any other dignitaries who wished to be included to contact the artist without delay as the number of portraits was limited.

The actual moment immortalised in the work of art showed the Mayor standing on the Corner Stone and calling for three cheers. Facing him can be seen the Lord of the Manor, Joseph Feilden, Exchange Company directors Joseph Harrison, William Stones and James Dickinson, and company secretary Thomas Crook Ainsworth, among others, while several leading ladies can be picked out on their viewing platform - a veritable pictorial Who's Who of the leading notables in Blackburn at that time. In actual fact, not all the notables in the painting were actually present at the laying of the stone and it was later said that certain individuals - including MP William Henry Hornby - who were keen to have their faces included had paid £10 to the artist for the privilege.

The finished painting was put on display in the main Exchange Hall when the building opened three years later, although it had a chequered history over the next century. After only a couple of years, it was moved for temporary display in the town's Public Library, and then by early 1869 it was back at the Exchange Hall.

In June 1875, it was reported that the council's Free Library Committee wanted to obtain the artwork for permanent display in the new Library and Museum which had just opened in Library Street. The painting's ownership

CHAPTER 4 — A RED-LETTER DAY

was then debated at a full council meeting, with some members stating that it was the property of the Exchange Company, while others argued that as it had actually been subscribed for by various prominent councillors and businessmen in the town it was actually the property of Blackburn Corporation.

The debate ended with a motion being passed that the council would attempt to obtain the painting for the museum, although its subsequent whereabouts over the next 100 years or so are something of a mystery. It is thought likely that it may have been moved to the Town Hall, perhaps for display in one of the council offices, although no record has come to light of its actual location, and then at some stage it was transferred to the Technical College.

In a curious aside, the Blackburn Standard of 7th April, 1894, reported that Blackburn photographer Leslie Shawcross had produced a "high-class" photo of the Laying of the Foundation Stone which had clearly been taken from the Sherwood painting. It was being displayed in the Church Street shop window of decorator W.H. Cunliffe, and was "claiming a large amount of public attention", possibly because many of the people depicted were well-known members of local families. In a follow-up report about council business on 6th October, the Standard said the Free Library Committee had accepted an enlarged photograph of the painting, the gift of the directors of the Exchange Company.

Whatever had happened to the actual work of art in the subsequent years, it was re-discovered in the 1960s, when it was found stuffed out of sight and gathering dust behind lockers in the old Technical College building in Blakey Moor. The story was told in the Looking Back section of the Lancashire Telegraph in March 2006 after the newspaper reported that the painting had been cleaned and re-framed for an exhibition at Blackburn Museum and Art Gallery.

Reader Ray Holt, who worked for the town's Education Authority with responsibility for school furnishings, wrote in to say that in the 1960s his department had received a letter from Canada. He went on: "It was from a lady who was a distant relative of someone in the painting and she said that she had obtained information that it was stored behind students' lockers in the old Tech.

- 46 -

"A couple of us went across there and eventually we found it behind some wooden lockers down a corridor. Though it's a massive painting, it was completely hidden. It was dirty and so dark behind the lockers that we had to borrow a torch from one of the caretakers. At first, I thought it showed some ship's rigging, but that turned out to be the builders' scaffolding. We shoved it back and went to the Library, told them where it was and asked them to reply to the letter. We were glad to hand the matter over to them."

Fortunately, the painting - which has been described as one of the town's greatest treasures - is now permanently on view at the Museum and Art Gallery, along with the ceremonial trowel and mallet.

# CHAPTER 5
# A SETBACK

**With** the day of celebrations behind them, the builders resumed construction and the Exchange Company began looking forward to the day when it could be opened for business. It appears that progress was slower than the company had expected, but things picked up in April when Farrell sub-let the stone work to Gabbott & Son, of Liverpool.

The work was marred by a serious accident in late January 1864. The Preston Herald reported that labourer John Mellody, of Moor Street in Blackburn, was carrying a large stone on scaffolding about 16 feet from the ground when his foot slipped and he fell off, taking the stone with him.

No bones were broken, but as he hit the ground, the stone struck him on the head, causing a severe head wound. It was a rare hiccup in the actual building work.

By the autumn of 1863, however, it was becoming clear that - presumably due to the continued economic misery occasioned by the Cotton Famine - the hoped-for number of shares in the enterprise would not all be taken up. As a consequence, a hasty revision of the building plans was put into effect, with construction being limited to the right-hand wing containing the main meeting room and private offices, plus the central tower, while work on the left-hand wing, which was due to house the News Room and other communal rooms, was put in abeyance until more prosperous times.

This decision was a disappointing one for the 512 subscribers to the existing Town Hall Exchange News Room and at their annual meeting in November 1863, their committee warned that it would be "a serious, if not fatal, defect" to the success of the new edifice if the separate News Room was not proceeded with. It was resolved that the surplus funds of the Town Hall meeting room amounting to around £1,900 should be invested in Exchange Company shares in the hope that the full building scheme could be resurrected.

At the beginning of 1864, it was announced that Blackburn Corporation had taken out a three-year lease at £35 a year on the Catholic Hall to house the borough's free lending library and museum pending a decision on finding a permanent home for these amenities. They had previously been based in cramped premises in the Town Hall which had long been considered to be inconvenient. In fact, there had been rumours and speculation as early as 1860 that the library could be housed in the Exchange building. The British and Irish Magnetic Telegraph Company also transferred their office from the railway station to one of the ground floor shops at about the same time, although the proposed incorporation of a new post office into the main Exchange had not been proceeded with.

At the fourth annual meeting of the Exchange Company in May 1864, it was confirmed that the plans for the delayed left-hand wing of the building had been referred back to the architect for reconsideration. Notwithstanding the lease of the Catholic Hall for the library, it was suggested that there could be a revision of the News Room part of the proposals to include this property as soon as possible, with director Joseph Harrison, presiding, arguing that consideration of the hall's incorporation into the revised scheme had become necessary.

After almost a decade, the town's Free Library finally vacated the former Catholic Hall in June 1874 when the Borough Council opened their new Library and Museum in Library Street. Later in the year, the Church Institute took over the Catholic Hall as a lecture room and meeting place until November 1885, when the Exchange Company began advertising it as a lecture hall for hire, usually under the name of the Exchange Assembly Hall to differentiate it from the main hall. It was increasingly used alongside the main hall to host smaller events or act as an overspill room, being connected directly to the Exchange by a passage.

In the late 1870s, the space between the Catholic Hall and the hotel was redeveloped by the Exchange Company with construction of a three-storey building with shops fronting Town Hall Street and another large first-floor assembly hall to provide even more space for meetings and other events. In the 1920s, local entrepreneur Tony Billington took the lease of this hall and obtained a licence for music and dancing, and in the 1930s a sprung dancefloor was added. For 80 years, it was at the heart of Blackburn's nightlife as Tony's Empress Ballroom, until its closure in 2003.

One major consequence of the cutback in the plans for the intended News Room wing of the main Exchange was that the Feilden's Arms was saved from demolition. Instead, it was renamed the Exchange Hotel and reopened in 1864 as a public house and for paying guests, with former joiner and builder William Byrom as the licensee. However, for whatever reason, Byrom soon appeared to be experiencing financial difficulties and on 2nd September, he was declared a bankrupt at a court hearing in Manchester. The following day, the hotel licence was transferred to a new tenant, Thomas Latham, 76, who was reputedly the oldest licensed victualler in the borough.

Mr Latham, a staunch Conservative, was well-known throughout the country for his skills at training dogs for coursing, and it is claimed that he had held 46 different public house licences in his long career behind the bar. Sadly, he died on 21st May, 1866, aged 79, and his widow Agnes took over the licence. As building work was nearing completion in early July 1864, a traditional "rearing supper" was laid on at the hotel for more than 40 labourers, at which "customary loyal and patriotic toasts" were given, with glasses raised to the Exchange Company and the directors, to the architect, the contractors and to "the town and trade of Blackburn". According to the Blackburn Standard "numerous songs and recitations were given, and a most convivial evening was spent".

The newspaper reported that it had been hoped that the new Cotton Exchange would be ready for opening on 1st July, but the delays meant that it would be at least October before it was finished. Nevertheless, the Standard decided to take the opportunity to give readers a fulsome description of the work. It said: "The building is in the Gothic style of architecture, and will contain a magnificent room with 7,000ft of floor space, besides fireproof offices and rooms for business purposes.

"The chief entrance is via an octagon hall, with a very handsome groined stone roof, surmounted by a tower or dome, and direct access is at once obtained to the large Exchange room. The whole structure, when completed, will present a frontage of 130 yards, and be the noblest and best adapted range of Exchange buildings in the provinces. Too much praise cannot be given to the architect for the elegant design and excellence of the internal arrangements."

A detailed factual 900-word description of the newly-opened Exchange was given in the 2nd June, 1865, issue of the trade paper Building News, full of architectural terms about groins, finials, gables, pinnacles, buttresses and the like, and a few highlights are perhaps worthy of a mention here. The article reported that externally, the building was entirely of locally-sourced stone except for the piers and arching of the basement, plus internal walling, which was of brick and cement. There was a combination of Longridge stone for the tower and vestibule as well as the complete frontage, with Darwen stone for the back and flank and Burnley stone for the internal dressings.

The reviewer wrote that the principal front in King William Street was divided into alternate bays of double-light windows and bay windows rising from the ground. Each main angle had a buttress and a large octagonal turret surmounting the parapet. Internally, the Exchange Room was divided into four equal parts, with an open timber hammer-beam roof carried on 18 cast iron pillars, 40ft high at the centre, and 23ft 6in high at the sides, with tracery spandrels and carved stone corbels springing from the side walls.

The roof panels were divided by moulded ribs and boarded with Baltic pine, slightly stained and well varnished, while the lower portion of the roof above the longitudinal arches was enriched by a double-moulded and perforated frieze passing entirely around. The floor was of pitch pine, except for a margin of four feet around the entire room, which was in Minton tiling, which was also used in the vestibule.

One particularly interesting point in the Building News review regards the tower, being constructed of two stages. The bottom portion was described as consisting of two deeply recessed arches around the main entrance doors, with the second stage having three-light windows with arched and tracery heads, separated by weathered buttresses. The paper went on to point out that the tower was intended to have a third stage, but this had been left for completion at a later date - presumably when funds could be found to demolish the hotel and build the intended left-sided wing.

The October date which had been proposed for the opening came and went, but at the next annual meeting of the Town Hall Exchange News Room on 25th November, there was speculation that the new Cotton Exchange would open for business on the first Wednesday of the new year. Chairman Thomas Crook Ainsworth told the meeting that there had been a big increase of 139 in the number of subscribers to the News Room in the previous 12 months, and the total now stood at 651. He said this was far too many to be comfortably housed at the Town Hall and so he was looking forward to the impending move across the road to the new building.

He also said he was confident that the accommodation and comfort provided would exceed those of any commercial building in the United Kingdom, and if the trade of the district at that time had been in "a more flourishing state" they could have had 800 or 1,000 members by now. Mr Ainsworth went on to say that when the Town Hall was finally vacated, the accumulated funds of the News Room amounting to £1,900, which had been invested in the Exchange Company, would be paid over to the Blackburn Infirmary and other charitable institutions in the town, as previously agreed by the committee.

## CHAPTER 6
# OPEN AT LAST

It was another four months or so before the Cotton Exchange officially opened on Wednesday, 3rd May, 1865, and in contrast to the lavish celebrations that had accompanied the laying of the Foundation Stone, it was a decidedly low-key affair with no ceremony at all. According to reports in the local press, this was because the Exchange Company had found it impossible to secure the services of a leading dignitary to perform the official opening.

Among others, they had approached the Earl of Derby of Knowsley Hall, three times the Prime Minister of Great Britain, Spencer Cavendish, heir to the Duke of Devonshire, who was a leading Liberal politician and captain of the Duke of Lancaster's Own Yeomanry, and Lord Winmarleigh, MP for North Lancashire and an active supporter of efforts to relieve the poverty in the town caused by the Cotton Famine. Apparently, they all declined the invitation.

The first event to take place in the new Exchange Hall was actually staged seven days earlier, on the evening of Wednesday, 26th April, when a musical concert was held, with all proceeds going to the town's new Infirmary. The Blackburn Times reported that the evening could be considered as the "grand opening" as the official day was to be so low-key. The room was packed with standing room only for performances of Mendelssohn's Violin Concerto, Beethoven's Kreutzer Sonata, and a programme of songs from vocalists Madame Parepa, Miss Palmer and J.G.Patey, with musical accompaniment from violinist Herr Joachim with Madame Arabella Goddard on pianoforte. Madame Goddard was rapturously applauded for her pianoforte solos on The Last Rose of Summer and Home Sweet Home, while Madame Parepa encored with I Dreamt I Dwelt in Marble Halls.

Commenting on the concert, and on the opening of the building, the Blackburn Times went overboard in praise of the evening, writing: "A stranger passing would suppose that the ecclesiastical structure with its stained glass windows was a church or chapel, and would need to be informed that the building was an Exchange, sacred to cotton and cotton pieces.

"The formal opening is to take place next Wednesday, with as little formality as possible, but the grand opening was on Wednesday night with a concert under the direction of Mr David Johnson, who for the energy and the ability he displayed in bringing the best concert ever held in Blackburn to a successful conclusion, deserves special thanks."

Remarking that the Sherwood painting, Laying the Foundation Stone, was now on display near the entrance and was an attraction to the hall, the newspaper added: "Looking down the vast room, one could not help feeling thankful that a place has at last been built in which meetings and concerts may be held without damage to the constitutions of those who speak and sing, as has been the case with the Town Hall, in consequence of the deficiency in its acoustical properties."

The acoustics were also commented on when the Exchange Company held their annual shareholders' meeting on the afternoon of 3rd May, following the official opening. Perhaps surprisingly, this was not held in the Exchange Hall but at the offices of solicitor and company secretary Thomas Crook Ainsworth round the corner in Town Hall Street. A report on the completion of the project was presented, and before turning to financial matters, the directors said they were glad to be able to report that the recent musical evening had confirmed that the hall's acoustic properties, and its adaptation for such purposes, were highly satisfactory, and warranted a hope that a considerable revenue could be derived in future from such events.

Shareholders were told that it was not possible at that time to give a full account of the total cost of the work as they were still awaiting some figures from the architect, but a total of 1,117 shares had been taken up, from which £10,707 had been paid out, leaving arrears of £463. There was also a mortgage of £1,050 outstanding on the purchase of the short-lived Catholic Hall. However, arrangements had been made to borrow £5,000 which would allow the company to pay off the mortgage debt, complete an outstanding payment on the purchase of the hotel, and discharge any final balance owing to the contractor, Mr Farrell.

The report added: "Your directors think that when the cost of the building is compared with the revenue that may be expected from the subscriptions of members, rents of offices, occasional use of the large room, etc, they will be warranted in proceeding with the left wing of the building for a News Room, thus completing that portion of the undertaking which is intended for the comfort and convenience of the subscribers."

Sadly, the plans for the left wing were never to be resurrected, and space had to be found for the Exchange's News Room by a reshuffle of the internal arrangements of offices and other rooms facing Town Hall Street, including the adjoining hotel. But with more than 600 of those subscribers eligible to make use of the building, the Cotton Exchange now settled down to its day-to-day focus on the commercial interests in the town, and the weekly get-togethers by merchants and traders engaged in the business of buying and selling cotton products and woven cloth resumed in the place that had at last been specially built for them, the main Exchange Hall.

The first few weeks were marred by one sour note at a meeting of the Town Council in early September, when the Clerk read out a letter from a neighbouring shopkeeper, Thomas Boardman, drawing attention to an alleged encroachment of the new building on to the footpath in King William Street. The complainant said the building had wrongly taken up 2ft 8in of the public pavement at its widest point, and he called upon the council to demand that the Exchange Company should restore the path to its original extent.

Councillor J. Livesey said Mr Boardman had spoken to him about the matter three or four times, but he had since spoken to a representative of the Exchange Company, who denied there had been any encroachment. Another councillor said he had heard that Mr Boardman was going to make an application to erect boxes on the pavement outside his shop unless the council dealt with the matter. The Mayor, Councillor James Thompson, said that if there had been any encroachment, the Exchange Company were unaware of it. After some further discussion, it was decided to refer the letter and the plans of the building to the Highways Committee.

Four months later, in early December, the footpath was the subject of more complaints to the council about obstructions due to traders congregating outside the Exchange entrance to carry out their business, perhaps in an unconscious echo of the dealings outside the Old Bull a decade and more earlier. It was reported that the police has been instructed to prevent a recurrence.

While the Cotton Exchange's commercial facilities were an undoubted asset to the business people of Blackburn, the building also quickly assumed a very important role in the social fabric of the town, providing for the first time a large space in which the townsfolk could gather for musical concerts, dinners, lectures, auctions, trade exhibitions, bazaars, fairs, dances, wedding celebrations, children's shows, charity fund-raisings and political meetings. As the Blackburn Times had hinted in the review of the opening night concert, the only comparable venue for most of these events was the Town Hall, which lacked the space - and the acoustics - now on offer across the road. The other large venue for public events in the town was the Theatre Royal on Ainsworth Street, which mostly staged theatrical performances.

One of the first times the Cotton Exchange was used for a public performance after the opening was in April 1867, when a lecture was given by a visiting New Yorker, Lorenzo Fowler, who was described in the local press as "the eminent phrenologist". It should perhaps be said that at the time, the much-derided pseudo-science of phrenology was all the rage on both sides of the Atlantic, and was based on the idea that by measuring bumps on a human skull you could predict mental traits such as intelligence, memory, compassion, judgement, attention and perception.

According to a report in the Preston Herald, Mr Fowler concluded his talk on "Formation of Character" by closely examining and commenting on the heads of two members of the audience. The newspaper took great delight in reporting: "One of these persons was the notorious William Gregson, teetotal lecturer and common councilman of the borough of

Blackburn, whose cranium was manipulated and explained to the intense delight of the audience."

Councillor Gregson was described by Mr Fowler as a man who knew how to work hard, but also knew when to stop. He was also said to be a naturally polite and at the same time, "a very positive man". Thanking the phrenologist for his insights, the councillor urged the young people present to read Mr Fowler's works "if they wanted to become men". It later transpired that he had met the phrenologist on previous occasions and willingly took part in the act.

The next major event at the Exchange came in January 1869 when the celebrated American comic actor, writer and playwright Howard Paul and his English wife, actress and singer Isabella Hill, gave a concert to a packed hall. Mrs Paul was famous for her musical impersonations, her comic roles and her involvement in the first Gilbert and Sullivan operas.

But it was the evening of Monday, 19th April, which perhaps set the seal on the Exchange as a major entertainment venue when novelist Charles Dickens visited on his "farewell" reading tour of the country. Dickens had toured Britain several times over the previous decade giving readings from his novels to entranced audiences, and he had visited the Theatre Royal only two years earlier in April, 1867. But with his health failing, he embarked on one last tour starting in October 1868 in which he was contracted to visit 75 towns and cities before a dozen readings in and around London.

The Blackburn Standard reported that for one shilling each, an Exchange Hall audience "comprising the elite of Blackburn and its vicinity" heard him give a full reading of A Christmas Carol and Bob Sawyer's Party from his first novel, The Pickwick Papers.

According to the Standard, Dickens looked to be in excellent health and those present "testified their admiration of his transcendent abilities as an author, an elocutionist and an accomplished mimic by hearty plaudits again and again renewed".

What neither the newspaper nor any members of the audience could probably have known was that Dickens's health was seriously fading and, indeed, it is said that he had suffered a mild stroke only the previous evening after a reading in Chester. Affected by giddiness and fits of paralysis, he collapsed again just three days later in Preston before he could give his next performance - and on a doctor's advice, the rest of the tour was cancelled.

The Exchange reading was the last public performance that Dickens ever gave outside London. He returned to his home in Kent to start work on his last (unfinished) novel, The Mystery of Edwin Drood, and then, after taking medical advice, he agreed to a final short series of readings in the capital beginning in January, 1870. He suffered another stroke at his home on 8th June and died the following day, aged 58.

Other early visitors to the Exchange were the celebrated Siamese twins Chang and Eng, from Thailand, who toured the world before settling in the United States, the 7ft 9in tall Canadian woman Anna Swan, known as "the Giantess" and described on posters as "the largest woman in the world", and Zoebida Luti, from the Black Sea region of Russia, a circus performer and magician who was said to be able to produce items including flowers, birds, and flags from thin air.

# CHAPTER 7

# SHOW TIME

The directors of the Exchange Company were clearly happy with the regular events in the main hall which brought in a substantial revenue and no doubt enhanced their prestige in the town. A slow but steady increase in the number of News Room subscribers and the letting of various offices, plus the basement shops fronting King William Street, also ensured a regular income.

The facilities were not welcomed wholeheartedly by everyone, however. The Blackburn Standard on 27th September 1870 printed a letter from "A Reader and Worker" claiming that the Exchange Hall was "a dark and cheerless place for business", while the separate space which had been set aside as the News Room was dirty and un-whitewashed and to call it a reading room was a misnomer. He said it should perhaps be better termed a "gossiping room" as it was regularly occupied by a three or four individuals whose "babbling and cackling" would soon drive away anyone thinking of using the facilities for reading. He also complained that the staging of exhibitions and concerts in the Exchange Hall attracted noisy crowds and blocked the entrance for subscribers.

A perusal of press cuttings from the 1870s, 1880s and 1890s shows a wide variety of social and cultural events bringing the people of the town into the Cotton Exchange for entertainment, with a Gypsy Ball, a Hypnotic Seance, a Toy Show and Carnival, a Masonic Dance, a Horticultural Show, a Yeomans' Ball, a Pottery Sale, a "Diorama of New Zealand", and a Shakespearean recital of The Merchant of Venice being just a small cross-section of the varied fare on offer in these years. In adverts and in references in the local press, the main hall and related facilities were increasingly being described as the "Exchange Assembly Rooms" with the reference to "Cotton" being dropped.

In June 1872, the Exchange was chosen as the venue for a practice demonstration by the town's Fire Brigade. Watched by an audience of local dignitaries and curious members of the public, the exercise began by the fixing of hoses to standpipes in King William Street before 90ft jets of water were trained on the tower, which was supposedly the seat of the blaze. Ladders were thrown up against the building, and firemen were also called to "rescue" volunteers trapped in the next-door hotel and bring them to the ground in safety. At the conclusion of the exercise, the brigade marched off in formation back to the fire station.

In December 1874, there was entertainment of a different kind when Sir Charles and Lady Halle, founders of the world-famous Halle Orchestra, gave one of their celebrated pianoforte and violin recitals, and other major stars of the day to bring in a crowd included the music hall singer and comedian Albert Chevalier, known as "The Coster King", and the composer and organist W. H. Jude with his "Musical Tramp Abroad" show. Another celebrated visitor was the American explorer and writer Henry Morton Stanley, who told the story of his rescue of the lost Scottish explorer Dr David Livingstone in east

Africa in his lecture "Through the Dark Continent" in November 1878.

In February 1877, the Exchange hosted a week-long visit by Annie De Montford, who was described in the press as "the greatest mesmerist in the world". The daughter of a Leicester mill worker, she assumed the stage name and claimed to use "mental magnetism" - hypnotism - to put members of the audience into a trance and to act in odd ways, to the obvious amusement of everybody else in the hall. She toured Britain for 10 years from 1872 with advertising posters for her performances claiming that "her mind governs the world" although an investigation of her act by an American reporter apparently revealed that she used stooges and some fans became so obsessed with her that they followed her around and volunteered to be her willing subjects night after night.

A second visit to the Exchange by a stage mesmerist 10 years later in September 1887 caused a near-riot which made headlines in national newspapers. The American Anna Fay was performing a week-long series of "spirit demonstrations" which apparently included tables and chairs floating in mid-air and flowers suddenly materialising out of nowhere. But when the lights were turned down and what appeared to be an illuminated figure of a woman floated across the hall, one man who had been suspicious of the stunt at a previous performance stood up and thrust a sharp hooked stick into the floating body and brought it to the ground. It was found to be nothing more than an inflated linen bag on which a figure had been painted, to which was attached a string to draw it rapidly above the audience along a very fine wire. Several members of the audience erupted in fury at the deception, and police had to be called to clear the crowd.

One show that went down rather better with townsfolk in September 1884 was a three-day visit by Callender's Coloured Minstrels, who were said to be the most popular troupe of black performers in the US - though it is doubtful that their programme of comic antics and songs from the slave plantations of the American South would nowadays gain the sort of affirmation offered by the Preston Herald reviewer who hailed "an agreeable couple of hours' amusement". Even less likely to find favour today was a performance in March 1890 by the Livermore Brothers' World-Renowned Court Minstrels, an English minstrel band who performed in blackface with a similar selection of American song and dance routines.

On 9th May, 1888, Blackburn was honoured with its first royal visit when Prince Albert Edward, the Prince of Wales, and Princess Alexandra accepted an invitation from the town council to lay the foundation stone for the new Technical College in Blakey Moor. As the royal procession was to be routed along King William Street for the couple to take lunch at the Town Hall, the Exchange Company seized on the chance to cash in ahead of the big day, placing advertisements in the local press offering to rent out the use of the large bay windows overlooking the street - which no doubt would have afforded a "bird's eye" view of the visitors. Businesses and homeowners with large windows or gardens elsewhere along the royal route also advertised "spaces to let".

The Exchange Hall was regularly booked for annual dinners and social gatherings by local workers' groups and trade associations, including postmen, railway workers, masonic lodges, and the Rifle Volunteers - and not forgetting the cotton trade, where it was also the usual venue for socials and dances for the Federated Cardroom Operatives and Spinners, with 400 people normally in attendance.

One type of event that appeared regularly at the Exchange during these years was the charity bazaar. Sales of donated and second-hand goods were held for local churches, schools, overseas missions, Blackburn's Orphanage and Ragged School and other good causes, as well as general fund-raising events for the town's poor. In February 1885, the entire hall was given a makeover for a grand Venetian fair to raise money for the building of St Matthew's Church at Higher Audley.

In January 1895, kind donors named only as "Mr and Mrs Baines and family" laid on a Punch and Judy show and tea at the Exchange for 90 children from the Blackburn Workhouse, while in August 1896, the Band of the 6th Dragoon Guards, based at Preston Barracks, gave two concerts of sacred music to raise money for the Railway Servants' Orphanage. For several years in the 1880s and 1890s, the hall was also the venue for the council's annual Christmas dinner for the town's poor.

In November 1894, East Lancashire Cricket, Bowling and Tennis Club held a four-day fundraising function in the hall in a bid to raise £800 to pay off debts and build a new pavilion and other improvements at Alexandra Meadows in West Park Road. Similarly, in March 1895, Blackburn Rovers FC held a three-day bazaar opened by the town's MP,

William Coddington, owner of the town's Ordnance and New Wellington cotton mills, in a bid to raise funds to pay off a £1,400 debt which had been accrued by the club due to the compulsory move they had recently made from their Leamington Street ground to Ewood Park.

An interesting sideline to this function was that the Exchange Hall was decorated with coloured electric lights following the recent opening of Blackburn's new coal-fired electric generating station in Jubilee Street. In a report in the progress of the new power source, headed "Dazzle is the watchword of the age", the Blackburn Standard reported that the power station had the capacity for up to 10,000 lamps and public lighting was already being installed throughout the town centre including King William Street, Sudell Cross, Richmond Terrace, Victoria Street, Church Street, parts of Northgate and Darwen Street. The gas lighting in the Exchange was replaced by electric lighting at around the same time.

Blackburn Rovers, incidentally, booked the Exchange for at least two annual general meetings in the 1890s, while the hall was regularly used for other serious events, including annual meetings of the Thwaites Brewery shareholders and the 1895 annual conference of the English Church Association and Protestant League. In October 1892 the Scottish MP Keir Hardie, founder of the Labour Party and later the first Labour Prime Minister (1906-08), addressed two meetings in the Exchange Hall at the invitation of the Blackburn branch of the Social Democratic Federation on the subject of "The Liberals versus the Labour Party". The Exchange was also the venue for counting the borough's votes at some General Elections in the years before 1900.

One other type of entertainment to be held regularly in the Exchange during these years offered townsfolk a foretaste of the sort of spectacle of light that could be enjoyed in the hall for more than 80 years through the next century - not yet cinema performances, but the "magic lantern" show. In this innovative new technology, images from slides were thrown on to a big screen by a light generated by throwing a flame on to a glass cylinder containing quicklime - hence the term "limelight".

Mentioned briefly earlier was a "New Zealand diorama" which was staged at the hall for a week in November 1881. Scenes painted on glass panels illuminated by gas lamps from the rear showed a fire which destroyed Kororareka, the whaling port which had been established by the first British settlers on the North Island in the early 18th Century, plus views of Mount Cook, the cities of Christchurch, Wellington and Dunedin and lastly a panel representing a ship moving across the sea in a snowstorm with the hills of New Zealand in the background.

In March 1885, the Rev S J Perry, Director of the Stonyhurst College Observatory, gave a lecture to a packed hall on new discoveries by astronomers about the solar system which he illustrated with illuminated slides of planets and other celestial objects. Several visits to the Exchange were also made by a touring show known as Poole's Myriorama (an invented word to mean "moving image") which presented large illuminated painted canvas scenes of dramatic events including the Battle of Waterloo and the Charge of the Light Brigade which moved at speed across the stage on rollers.

In November 1896 the hall was the venue for a performance by Whiffly Puncto's Magic Lantern Show. According to the Blackburn Standard, the slides on view produced striking contrasts between the squalid slums of Manchester and Liverpool and the extravagances of the wealthy classes, as depicted in views of Eaton Hall, the Cheshire seat of the Duke of Westminster, and the Houses of Parliament. The display was accompanied by a series of popular tunes of the day performed by a pianist.

The introduction of electricity in Blackburn has already been touched on, and actual cinema performances, albeit of a primitive nature, were also staged in the Exchange Hall in the last couple of years before 1900. While pioneering equipment to produce moving images on a screen had already gained the term "cinematograph", the shortened version of the word was not yet in common use, and the show staged in the hall on 5th February 1898 was described as a performance of "Animated Photographs".

Possibly the first-ever cinema performance to be held at the Exchange, it was staged by the proprietors of Nestles Condensed Milk and Sunlight Soap to show off the new technology of moving pictures while also promoting their products. A packed programme with brief scenes of 40 varied events on more than 1,000ft of photographic film was screened, including Queen Victoria's Diamond Jubilee procession, Henley Regatta, an Army review at Aldershot and a bullfight in Madrid, all with musical accompaniment.

Another early cinema performance at the Exchange had a more local flavour. On 24th September 1898, one of Britain's earliest film-makers, Welshman Arthur Cheetham, set up his camera behind the goal at what appears to be the Darwen End at Ewood Park to record scenes from Blackburn Rovers' First Division match against West Bromwich Albion.

According to the British Film Institute, it is possibly the earliest football match ever to be preserved on film, and it led a programme of short films screened at the Exchange on 19th October, 1898. Just one minute long, it is claimed to show two of Rovers' goals in a 4-1 victory, although it is case of "a blink and you've missed 'em" in the primitive and grainy black and white footage which can be viewed for free on the BFI's website and on YouTube. The Blackburn Standard review of the show was headed "Exciting moment at a cinematograph show" - although the excitement had little to do with the football film. As the hall was plunged into darkness to begin the screening there was suddenly a "crashing, rushing sound" from the rear, followed by cries of alarm from people in the body of the auditorium who started to make a stampede for the exits.

As the lights were hastily turned up, it was revealed that the commotion had been caused by a crowd of latecomers bursting through the barriers at the rear in a bid to claim their seats. Apparently no damage was done and nobody was hurt and the audience soon settled down to watch the show. The Standard added: "The football film, which is claimed to be the largest and most successful yet taken, gave a capital idea of portions of the game, particularly of the scoring of two of the Rovers' goals, and the audience cheered them cordially."

# CHAPTER 8
# IN DECLINE

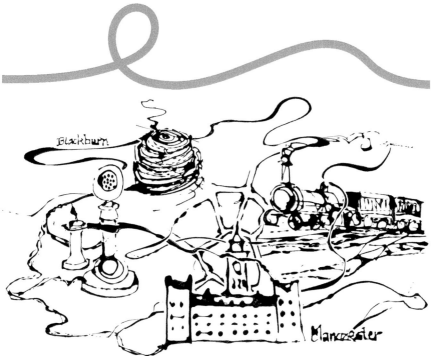

**Alongside** all the various social and cultural activities, the Exchange Hall was also, of course, fulfilling its primary function of providing a place for the town's cotton manufacturers and traders to conduct their business. However, the building's use for this commerce became less and less important in the last couple of decades of the 19th Century. This was not because of any decline in Blackburn's industrial output during these years. Far from it, in fact. The town's weaving mills had never been busier and in 1890 it was estimated that one-eighth (12.5%) of all the looms producing cotton cloth in Lancashire and surrounding counties could be found within the boundaries of the borough.

But this success paradoxically made the need for a local Cotton Exchange less important, not more so. The locally-owned businesses which had grown up and expanded through the early part of the century were mostly now successful on a nationwide level and, as such, could secure long-term contracts for their output with both clothing and cloth goods manufacturers and exporters. Much of this business was centred on the Royal Exchange in Manchester, and hence there was less need for merchants to come to Blackburn to see local manufacturers directly. Improved railway links and the introduction of the telephone in the latter years of the century were also contributory factors.

This decline in Blackburn's status as a centre for cotton trading was the subject of an address by Alderman Henry Harrison at the annual meeting of the Blackburn and District Chamber of Commerce in February 1891. Alderman Harrison, who was instrumental in the formation of the Chamber in the 1880s, was the youngest son of Alderman Joseph Harrison, who ran a loom-making foundry in the Nova Scotia area of the town in the mid-1800s and was one of the original directors of the Exchange Company.

When the family loom-making business was sold off, Henry invested in the spinning and weaving business, becoming the owner of Highfield, Chadwick Street and Witton Mills, employing about 1,000 people. He also had a warehouse in Manchester where he sold cloth directly, but in his address, he lamented the fact that he could no longer conduct this business successfully in his home town.

He said: "In the cotton trade there is at present only one distributing centre, Manchester to which Blackburn and all other towns engaged in the trade play second fiddle. In fact, Blackburn people help to swell the wealth of Cottonopolis at their own cost. Blackburn is a great feeder of Manchester, sending in to that town business it might keep for itself." Without mentioning the Cotton Exchange directly, he suggested that efforts should be made to rebuild the town's position as a major distributive as well as a manufacturing centre, with a consequent boost to a large number of subsidiary industries which were increasingly being "monopolised" by Manchester.

He continued: "For instance, in the making up and sale of cotton goods we should want dyers, finishers, warehousemen and packers, packing-case and box, sack and bag-makers, tinplate workers and a host of other occupations. Employment could be found in Blackburn for thousands of additional hands, both male and female, and the town would become, much more truly than it is now, the metropolis of the cotton trade."

It was an ambitious call, but one that largely went unanswered. Three years later, it seems the death knell was now sounding for the Exchange as a place for the mill owners to conduct any business. In an article in the Weekly Standard and Express in January 1894, on the recently-opened Manchester Ship Canal and the improvements it had brought to trade in Lancashire, and to Manchester in particular, the anonymous author wrote that Blackburn's commerce stood to gain from a lowering of transport costs for goods in and out. But on the debit side, he feared that developments around the canal in the Warrington area could lead to new cotton mills opening there to the detriment of the town, as the climate was just as suitable for weaving as in North-East Lancashire.

He questioned whether Blackburn and the surrounding area could withstand increased competition from new mills in the south-west of the county, particularly as the canal also brought them within easier reach of traders in Manchester, and he added: "Is it absolutely necessary that we should continue to do our business with the world through Manchester? Our local cotton market is completely dead, and the deserted Exchange is all we have left to tell of former days."

At the same time that the Exchange's importance for cotton trading was in decline, the use of the building as a News Room stocked with newspapers and periodicals for subscribers to read also became much less important. In fact, it can be argued that this function was out of date almost before the building opened, because four years earlier in 1861, the Government had abolished long-standing taxes on newspapers which had kept cover prices artificially high and circulations low.

Stamp duty was first imposed on news publications in 1712 as a way by the Government of the day to control sales and hence the dissemination of news to the general public about current affairs and Government activities, and the tax had steadily risen from one-halfpence to 4d per copy in the mid-1800s. By the time Queen Victoria came to the throne in 1837, it was only the income derived from advertising that enabled most daily and weekly newspapers to survive.

However, after Lord Palmerston became Prime Minister for the second time in 1859, one of his first acts was to abolish the stamp duty, freeing up the press and helping to launch a wide proliferation in newspapers and periodicals covering all points of view. The biggest daily newspaper in Britain, the Daily Telegraph, halved its price from 2d to 1d and doubled its circulation by 1862, and local newspapers saw similar surges in sales with cuts in their cover prices, enabling them to print many more copies to be sold on the streets and at factory gates. Contemporaneous improvements in education in the later years of the 19th Century meant that many more people were able to read and write, and customers of all social classes were eager to devour news about what was happening locally, nationally and around the world.

The Blackburn Standard, a weekly, was first published in 1835 with a cover price of seven pence, including 4d stamp duty, but by 1875, the price had fallen to one penny. From 1893, it widened its circulation from beyond the borough boundary and the name had changed to the Weekly Standard and Express. Bookseller James Walkden had printed only a few hundred copies of his first edition in 1835, but by 1882, the circulation was given as 10,000 copies a week. Rival weekly the Blackburn Times was first published in 1860, anticipating the end of stamp duty, while the area gained its first daily newspaper with the launch of the Northern Daily Telegraph in Blackburn in October 1886.

Inevitably, within a decade or so of the Cotton Exchange's opening, the number of subscribers to the News Room began to fall, and with it the Exchange Company's income from that source. This decline had almost certainly had a marked effect on the balance sheet by 1881, as the first moves were made to broaden the building's use with an application to the council to licence the building for theatrical and operatic performances.

This was granted, but it necessitated some expense in major improvements in the Exchange Hall to replace the small platform at the far end from the entrance with a full-sized stage measuring 53ft 6in wide and 26ft deep with six dressing rooms at the side. As the floor of the hall was perfectly level, the plans stipulated that the stage should be inclined towards the rear "at such an angle as to enable everyone to see" - which must have caused some problems for performers. The first show on the new stage was at the end of November 1881 by the Blackburn Literary Club. The stage and accessories

were described as "being of a very suitable nature and serve their purpose well". The performance included scenes from The Rivals by Richard Sheridan, and Cox and Box by Francis Burnand and Arthur Sullivan.

In the following years, it appears that the Exchange Company failed to persuade many touring theatrical productions to transfer to their building in preference to the town's regular drama and opera venue, the Theatre Royal, but the new stage did allow the Exchange to put on performances by large casts. Professor Andre's Alpine Choir, consisting of 20 singers in Swiss costume plus musicians, made several visits to the Exchange to present a mix of sacred and secular songs and musical sketches. And on Christmas Eve, 1885, the hall hosted the celebrated Carl Rosa Opera Company with a Grand Concert of Sacred Songs and Music with full band and chorus, possibly making full use of the entire stage for the first time.

In November 1889, one of the more unusual musical concerts was staged at the hall by the American Alice Shaw, who was billed as "La Belle Siffleuse", or "The Beautiful Whistler", in which she performed a range of tunes simply by whistling. A brief cylinder recording of one of her performances in London can be heard on the Exchange's website - possibly the earliest celebrity musical performance to be preserved.

# CHAPTER 9
# CAUSE FOR COMPLAINT

Into the 1890s, the Exchange Hall continued to stage all manner of social and cultural events, but the first signs that all was not well with the business came in late 1894 when the local press reported that a series of concerts, balls, bazaars and other events had been poorly attended. In November, a social and dance for members of the town's Cobden Club was deemed a flop when only 25 couples turned up, and a charity concert by the Band of the East Lancashire Regiment on 14th December was also declared "not a financial success". On 2nd January 1896, the local press reported that a disappointingly poor crowd turned out for a performance by Alfred Reisenauer, a pupil of the composer Franz Liszt and said to be one of the world's greatest pianists of the day.

Some months earlier, it was reported that the Blackburn Philharmonic Society had been wound up due to debts, which prompted one local commentator to lament that Blackburn could no longer consider itself "a musical town" - not because of a lack of musical events or the efforts of those who were keen to stage musical performances, but because local people were simply not prepared to pay the going rate to see such events at the Exchange.

The controversial remarks led to a series of letters to the Weekly Standard and Express both supporting and arguing against his comments. Most of the opinions expressed had no bearing on the success or otherwise of the Exchange as a venue, although one correspondent said the lack of a suitable hall with an organ was a major reason why Blackburn lost the chance to stage musical performances of the kind held regularly at the Public Hall in Preston.

He said Preston's venue also had splendid accommodation for a choir and an orchestra and he added: "Contrast that with our own catacomb-like Exchange Hall - dull, drab, repellant. Ugh!" His letter continued: "Do not let it be understood that I am in any way wishful to decry the provision the Exchange Company have made. One wonders what our public life in Blackburn in every department would have been like if they had not stepped into the breach, and provided us with such accommodation as we have. Unfortunately, we have long since outgrown their once-timely provision."

He suggested that the Exchange Company should make major changes to the hall, including a gallery, to make the interior brighter and more inviting, and he added: "We should then have a perfect public hall, and I am sure it would pay. Have they the necessary enterprise? They have the very best site in the town, and they need not fear any competition. With such a hall Blackburn would no longer take a back seat as compared with Preston. We might indeed take our rightful place as pioneers in musical education and progress."

There were also barbed comments from letter-writers to the local press that the Exchange Hall staged too many charity sales and bazaars, with the town's traders complaining that the volume of business at their annual Christmas Fair in the hall had suffered as a result.

In February 1895, one possible explanation for an about-turn in the hall's fortunes was voiced by the un-named author of the Passing Notes and Gossip column in the Weekly Standard and Express as he launched a full-blown verbal attack on the Exchange, describing it as "one of the dullest and most uncomfortable public buildings one can meet", blaming draughts of cold air which regularly plagued attendees at concerts. This was followed by further criticism in the newspaper from a contributor who said the draughts were caused by the constant opening and closing of the swing doors which led to the vestibule, and he suggested the problem should be tackled by erecting a screen between the back row of seats and the doors.

There was further trouble for the building in April 1895. A decade-and-a-half after the company had built a proper stage at considerable expense, the council refused permission for Blackburn Dramatic Society to stage two plays in the hall for the benefit of the town's Infirmary on safety grounds owing to the inadequacy of the exits. Six months later, the hall's dancing licence was up for renewal and the town's Chief Constable went to the Borough Court on 14th October to object to renewal for the same reason - that there were not sufficient means of exit from the building to meet "ordinary or extraordinary" occasions. He referred in particular to the stage area, which he said was often crowded with people at functions, and would be a source of danger in the event of a fire.

He applied for an adjournment, which was granted, so that the company could respond. Understandably, the court hearing led to a prompt planning application for permission to make changes to the exits, and on 23rd November, when the licence hearing resumed, the magistrates were told that the plans had been approved by the council, and the renewal of the dancing licence was granted, subject to the necessary alterations being carried out without delay.

Ironically, the work was under way in early February when a fire broke out in the stage area. Just before lunchtime, a "mild explosion" was heard caused by a leak of gas under the rear of the platform, and it set light to some woodwork. The Borough Fire Brigade attended within minutes to extinguish the flames, and very little damage was done, although it was said that it had been extremely fortunate that the fire had not occurred at night. Some wooden chairs were stacked close to the seat of the blaze, and if the flames had gained ground, they could have very quickly spread to the pitch-pine roof of the hall, with serious consequences. Possibly due to criticism of the amenities at the hall mentioned earlier, further structural alterations were now under consideration by the company to make it more suitable for musical concerts, including the erection of a gallery which would add around 300 extra seats, but at the next annual shareholders' meeting, there was no further discussion of the proposals and it was announced that they had been postponed.

However, the company did try to drum up more business by placing an advertisement in The Era, a national weekly newspaper which specialised in general theatrical information and news. It read:

"Centrally situated. Suitable for concerts, panoramas, entertainments etc. Licensed for music and dancing. Large stage. Will seat 1,200 to 1,500."

## CHAPTER 10
# AN UNCERTAIN FUTURE

**The** directors' reluctance to proceed with alterations was no doubt influenced by increased talk in the town in early 1897 that Blackburn needed some major public improvements, including a new town hall, as the office accommodation available in the existing building was becoming full up with the council's activities expanding to meet the ongoing increase in the population of the borough.

There had already been discussions in council circles and the local press about perhaps acquiring the Exchange and neighbouring buildings for this, although some commentators were totally opposed to the idea, with one letter-writer calling himself "Sanitas" arguing that the Exchange site was "cramped, irregular and unsuitable" for a new town hall. The council had also earmarked a site bounded by Northgate, Blakey Moor and Nab Lane for a possible suite of buildings including a public hall as well as council offices.

As debate continued in the town and in the Weekly Standard and Express, "Civicus" replied to "Sanitas" in favour of redeveloping the Exchange site. He wrote that it had "the immense advantage in a continuous approach of splendid perspective from the Market Place", and he said most people in the town passed it at least once a week. He said the same could not be said of the Blakey Moor site and, furthermore, the argument that the Exchange site was inferior because it was not symmetrical was irrelevant, pointing out that the Manchester Town Hall site was similar. "Civicus" also suggested that the site of the Exchange Hotel was suitable for a new public hall with perhaps a dome or tower on the corner.

Despite the arguments, there was no progress on the council's proposals for more than a year, and no progress, either, on any alterations to the Exchange. On the contrary, it was suggested in the press in early April 1898 that the Exchange Company would be willing to sell their site for demolition and redevelopment "at a price". It was reported that the Royal Mail were still looking for a suitable site for a new Post Office HQ, and it was surmised that the existing Town Hall could easily be adapted if the council decided to move.

At around the same time, a new threat to the Exchange's continued viability as a venue for concerts and other public events emerged with news that the council had granted permission for the building of a new theatre, the Palace, between Jubilee Street and Dandy Walk. It was reported that the structure would have seating for about 2,000 on three levels with side boxes. Just three months after the local press had published illustrated articles on the impressive accommodation that the new Palace Theatre could offer, there was a curious incident on 1st July 1898 which could have brought to a sudden end any debate about the Exchange's future.

The story unfolded in a news item in the following day's edition of the Northern Daily Telegraph under the headline: "The Exchange Hall luckily saved."

At around midnight, a policeman, PC Pattison, was walking along King William Street when he could smell smoke emerging from the vestibule at the Exchange. On looking through the glass panels of the door, he could see a quantity of wood and straw was on fire. He ran to the police station at the nearby Town Hall building and the Fire Brigade was called out. According to the Telegraph, they were on the spot "in an incredibly short space of time" and gained entrance to the building.

Making a quick search, the firemen were astonished to find four separate small, but distinct, fires were in progress. Two were close to each other in the vestibule but a third was in a storeroom and the fourth, consisting of a barrel stuffed with blazing straw, was under the stage. All four fires were quickly extinguished, but "the curious part of the affair", according to the Telegraph report, was that not long before the PC spotted the fire, some 20 men had been at work in the hall itself.

For the previous few weeks, a trade exhibition had filled the Exchange, but it had concluded earlier that evening and the workmen had been engaged in packing away the exhibits for removal the following day. One of the workmen told the Fire Brigade he had been working at the back of the stage and at that time there was no sign of any fire.

"The fact that the fires occurred in four separate places gives an ugly aspect to the outbreak", said the Telegraph, "and this was considerably intensified by another discovery made this morning, when it was found on entering the Reading Room, which is at the opposite end of the building, that two distinct fires had been burning there. There is a large screen just inside the doorway which serves a double purpose as a draught protector and as a noticeboard on which are displayed the share lists, cotton reports etc for the information of the members. The fires seem to have started simultaneously on each side of the screen, but did not get much beyond the smouldering stage." The newspaper reported that police had begun an investigation into the fires but no conclusions could be drawn.

The Exchange Company quickly cleared up the small amount of damage caused by the mysterious fires and then affected something of a U-turn by announcing that major alterations to their building would be going ahead after all. Director James Hoyle told shareholders that the present stage would be removed and in its place would be a gallery capable of

seating about 350 people, with direct access to exit doors underneath. A new stage would be constructed at the opposite end of the hall above the main entrance with a bridge linking it to one of the assembly rooms which would form an ante-room or dressing room for performers. Two pillars which hindered views for spectators would also be removed.

This work was put in hand without delay and within three months the remodelled Exchange Hall was ready to reopen on Monday, 26th September. In addition to the changes outlined by Mr Hoyle, the hall had been completely redecorated and was now said to be "bright and cheerful", while along the centre of the room, the lighting had been improved with the installation of three vertical-flame ventilated sun lights said to be identical to those in Preston's Public Hall.

The remodelling, which had cost an estimated £1,000, had also increased the seating capacity by 500, including the 350 in the gallery, and the auditorium could now comfortably seat 2,000 people.

There had been one minor hiccup during the alterations when the council's Health Committee issued an abatement notice after the Medical Officer of Health had received complaints that the building's chimney had been "sending forth black smoke in such quantity as to be a nuisance".

One of the first shows to be staged following the reopening was a week-long booking by Mr and Mrs Victor Andre, who presented what was described in the Weekly Standard as "their Oriental and psychic sensation". The newspaper added: "Their entertainment is full of marvel and mystery, Mrs Andre's dream seances being especially remarkable." A number of lectures, bazaars, charity concerts and other events followed in the remaining months of the year, although complaints about the annoying draughts also resurfaced. Reporting on one concert in late November, the music reviewer of the Standard commented that they might as well have been outdoors as the atmosphere inside the hall was so cold.

The Exchange's future was called into question again in January 1889 when the Exchange Hotel was put up for auction. It was reported that a large number of brewers and others connected to the licensing trade gathered at the hotel as it was offered for sale fully licensed and with freehold. In addition to the bar parlour, snug, commercial room, bar and vault, kitchen and two pantries on the ground floor, there was a large billiards room (with two tables), two sitting rooms and a stock room on the first floor plus six bedrooms, a box room and a bathroom on the second floor. The bidding started at £4,000 and rose gradually to £8,000, but when no higher bids were offered, the auctioneer declared the property withdrawn.

If the move to sell the hotel had come as a shock to the town, a much bigger one was to follow less than six months later in early June when it was announced that a winding-up order had been issued for the Blackburn Exchange Company Limited. The directors may have been holding out for a decision by the council on what was to be done about the Town Hall, and whether the Exchange was seriously in consideration as a possible site for redevelopment. But the signs from the council had been negative, particularly as on 10th April, the council sub-committee dealing with the issue had ruled out a sale of the Town Hall to the Royal Mail due to a disappointing offer from the Treasury of only £30,000 for the building.

On 10th August, the council announced that a final decision had been reached on the future of the Town Hall. It had been decided not to move after all, but to gain the extra accommodation needed by moving the Police Headquarters and Sessions House (Magistrates Courts) from

the building, possibly to a new site on Northgate. With some further extensions at the rear, it would also be possible to create a new Assembly Room with shops underneath, and this also ruled out any suggestion of erecting a new Assembly Room and shops on the site of the Exchange.

On 23rd December, 1899, theatrical newspaper The Era carried a notice of the sale by private treaty of the freehold estate of the Blackburn Exchange Company Limited. It stated: "The property includes the Exchange Hall, having accommodation for 2,000 people, with Artistes' Dressing and other rooms adjoining, Shops, Offices and Reading Rooms, the Exchange Hotel, one of the Leading Licensed Houses of the Town, and Shops, Warehouses, Assembly, Lecture, Ball, Supper and Ante rooms in Town Hall Street, a superficial area of 3,442 square yards - sold subject to all existing Leasings and Agreements, and to all Engagements and Hirings of the Public Rooms."

# CHAPTER II
# A NEW OWNER

The 20th Century dawned with a huge question mark hanging over the future of the Cotton Exchange. The first few months of 1900 went by without any news about what might happen to the building or the site. Across the road at the Town Hall, councillors and officials were still talking about the borough's need for a new assembly hall for public events, notwithstanding the suggestion that the remodelled Town Hall itself could provide the space needed - and some councillors continued to argue that a renovated Exchange, or a completely new building on the site, would fit the bill.

At the same time, council moves to redevelop the Northgate-Blakey Moor area were still actively under discussion. The site was currently occupied by a few narrow streets of rundown terraced houses which had been described by one observer as "a whole range of unsanitary rookeries" and proponents of the scheme argued that redevelopment of the area was becoming a necessity.

While councillors were still arguing over whether to go ahead, the Exchange remained the only hall of any size in Blackburn for the staging of musical concerts and other entertainments, and despite the demise of the old Exchange Company, a varied programme of musical concerts, trade exhibitions, lectures and meetings continued to attract townsfolk to the venue. Among the first events to be held in the Exchange while it was up for sale on 22nd January was a packed programme of classical music and operatic songs known as the Eccles Concert, arranged by a regular promoter at the hall, James Eccles.

The show was rapturously received by a large audience but led to some barbed criticism from the reviewer for the Weekly Standard and Express. He wrote that it was a pity the acoustic qualities of the hall failed to do justice to the performance of the well-known baritone Charles Copland, and - perhaps in ignorance of the fact that the building was for sale - he lamented: "Why cannot the Exchange authorities improve matters in this respect by spending some shillings on ways of improving this otherwise splendid building. It is positively painful under the present conditions."

The following month, a concert which had been arranged in the hall by a touring group known as the Ashdown Ballad Concerts was abandoned before it started when only 20 members of the public turned up. The music reviewer of the Weekly Standard and Express wrote: "Under such depressing conditions it was impossible for the artistes to appear. This is a strange contrast to Liverpool, Birmingham, Manchester and other towns where the Ashdown Concerts have proved such a financial and musical success. Can it be possible that the passion and desire for good high-class music is declining in local quarters?"

One of the biggest events to be held in the hall in 1900 was a Temperance Festival. By the end of the 19th Century, it is said there were around 200 beer shops and 250 hotels, inns and taverns in the borough of Blackburn, a fact which may or may not explain why the Exchange was the venue in

May for three days of celebrations of the joys and benefits of teetotalism. It was organised by the town's Band of Hope Union with the support of most Nonconformist chapels in the area, and there was such a big demand for tickets for the event on Thursday, 10th May, that an extra performance had to be arranged for the following week.

In fact, according to the Weekly Standard, the event attracted such interest from townsfolk that on the opening night people were in danger of being crushed in their eagerness to get into the hall. "The interest in the occasion was unique," wrote the reporter, "as there were almost as many anxious to obtain entry to the building as there were those who were lucky enough to obtain seats. Nearly an hour before the announced time of commencement, the main entrances were literally beseiged by a pressing, perspiring throng, whose excitement caused by the crush and desire to get a glimpse, was evident by the babel of tongues. It seems that by some reason, the tickets were undated, and every portion of the building was packed. The barriers dividing the room were unintentionally forced by the unavoidable pressure."

A programme of music and choral singing was accompanied by lectures on the "demon drink" and one of the highlights of the festival was the enthronement of Miss Nellie Highton as the May Queen accompanied by 16 Maids of Honour and another 50 children dressed as guardsmen, flower girls and in the various costumes of the home countries, the colonies and the Continent. Ahead of the event, the Weekly Standard and Express said: "There is no doubt that when all these are assembled on the large platform in the Exchange Hall, and the throne illuminated with electricity, the whole will form a very beautiful and memorable picture." In his address to open the festival, the Mayor, Councillor Edwin Hamer, said he was delighted to be invited to preside over such a magnificent gathering, and there were loud cheers as he said it was important that the town's young people should be raised "in the paths of Temperance". He praised the Band of Hope movement for their efforts to promote teetotalism, and he thanked them for their efforts in "training the young in all those moral virtues which would be a safe guide to them in their adult life".

On 19th February 1900, the town council met to formally consider the recommendations of the sub-committee regarding the future of the Town Hall, and it was agreed that the Northgate-Blakey Moor site should be

purchased for a new Public Hall, Police HQ and Magistrates Court and that the Town Hall should be extended to include a new Assembly Hall. The plans now acquired the official title of the Blackburn Improvement Scheme.

However, that was not quite the end of the matter. When details of the proposed scheme were published, there were rumblings in the town - expressed through letters to the press from people who were opposed to both the Northgate-Blakey Moor development on the grounds of cost, and to extensions to the Town Hall which would move the rear of the building closer to Victoria Street.

The objections were crystallised in the form of a pamphlet entitled "Blackburn's Improvement Problem" which was privately printed and circulated by the prominent letter-writer already encountered who signed himself "Civicus", although he was in reality fine art dealer and publisher Luke Slater Walmsley, of No 14 Preston New Road. His suggestion was to return to the idea of purchasing the Exchange Hall and to add to it all the property bounded by King William Street, Sudell Cross, Northgate and Town Hall Street and to build there a large assembly room which he dubbed the "Queen's Hall", He also proposed that the council should acquire the Northgate-Blakey Moor site as agreed but should build a new Town Hall there along with the Police HQ and courts.

With the town council having already made their decision, it seemed that "Civicus" and his pamphlet - and all the other objections - had been summarily dismissed. Before the end of the year, the council announced that architects had been employed to make suggestions for the design of the Blakey Moor site, and the likely outcome was a major building development on the lines previously suggested, linking a new Public Hall with seating for at least 2,500 people with a Magistrates Court, police headquarters, and other council offices. Negotiations began almost at once to buy up the many properties on the site but it would be a decade before it could be fully cleared and construction of the grand scheme could get under way.

In the meantime, as the year was nearing its end, news finally broke that Alfred Nuttall JP, proprietor of the Lion Brewery in Little Harwood and formerly Conservative councillor for the St Stephen's Ward, had purchased the Exchange from the trustees for £20,000. It was described as the largest business transaction to have taken place in the town for many years, and in an interview in the Weekly Standard and Express on 15th December, 1900, Mr Nuttall revealed that he had previously entered negotiations to buy the property from the Exchange Company two years previously, but had been unable to agree terms.

He had then embarked on a round-the-world tour, and it was only on his return that he learned that it was now up for sale. He said he had yet to decide what to do with the Exchange and the adjoining hotel, although local architects Briggs and Wolstenholme, of Richmond Terrace, had already been engaged and were working on some proposals for the total redevelopment of the site.

One idea was to turn it into three storeys of shopping space with rows of shops fronting King William Street and Town Hall Street surrounding a covered arcade with other shops facing inwards to it. In all, it was suggested that 42 separate shop premises could be created, mostly roofed over, and extending for 1,260ft in length, and the whole building would have a commanding elevation which would "add a great deal to the architectural beauty of the district". It was further proposed that above the shops on Town Hall Street there would be a suite of rooms approached by a grand staircase to comprise "assembly, crush, supper and cloakrooms with a kitchen and requisite accommodation".

The Weekly Standard and Express commented that if the proposals went ahead there was "not the slightest doubt the new buildings will considerably improve and brighten this important part of the town, and distribute the business places over a wider area." In the meantime, there were no moves to demolish any of the existing buildings, and Mr Nuttall said they would continue to be used for the same purposes as at present pending a final decision.

## CHAPTER 12
# BACK IN BUSINESS

**The** new year opened with the new owner of the Exchange hosting a free dinner for more than 300 of Blackburn's old folk, having distributed tickets to the most needy in the town. Just a few days into 1901, the guests were treated to roast beef, boiled mutton and plum pudding, followed by music, songs and comedy sketches by local artistes. Almost all the attendees were over the age of 70 and a few were in their late 80s. It was to be the first of an annual series of such dinners for the town's old people.

Before the end of January, another notice appeared in the theatres and concerts weekly The Era advertising the Exchange Hall for letting for entertainments, exhibitions and the like. One of the first uses to which the new owner put the Exchange was to stage the annual banquet of Blackburn and District Licensed Victuallers' Association on 27th February, with Mr Nuttall himself presiding.

In proposing continued prosperity for the association, the Lion Brewery chief clearly thought it would be an opportune time to speak up for the licensed trade in the town following recent criticism in the local press about drunken behaviour by townsfolk. He said the association's members did their best to conduct their business in the best possible way and they were not hostile to the views of magistrates or the Chief Constable where licensing matters were concerned. However, he spoke out against "petti-fogging charges brought forward by teetotal faddists and narrow-minded people".

Having been travelling abroad, Mr Nuttall may not have known that the hall had been the location for a Temperance Festival the previous May, but he was certainly aware of Mayor Edwin Hamer's own strident teetotalism. In proposing a toast to "the Mayor and Corporation", Mr Nuttall said he could not see eye-to-eye with the Mayor himself because of his very narrow views on the subject of alcohol, and he added: "It is my contention that anyone holding such narrow views and not knowing the world and the town as it ought to be known had no right to accept the position."

When his remarks were quoted in the local press, a storm of protest erupted, with churchmen, Temperance Society members and even a couple of town councillors condemning the brewer for his outburst. At a meeting of Blackburn's Teetotal Mission held a few days later, one speaker described Mr Nuttall's comments as "insolent and insulting", while another said that owing to the influence of brewers, Blackburn was "one of the most beer-ridden communities in the country".

Alcohol was again a contentious subject at the Exchange later in the year when a three-day bazaar was held there by St Alban's Roman Catholic Church. The Rev E. Melville Durbin, pastor of Leamington Road Baptist Church, told the Lancashire Evening Post how he had visited the bazaar on the Monday evening to find it dangerously crowded, and after fighting his way into the hall, he witnessed a sight he should never forget, and one that he did not hesitate to say was "a positive scandal and disgrace to any Christian church".

He said he was shocked to find a drinking bar at which intoxicating liquors were being supplied to men and women, and also to "mere lads and lasses". An illegal lottery was also being held with bottles of wine and spirits as the prizes, and there were what he believed to be roulette tables at which children were being encouraged to bet their pennies on the spin of the wheel. The pastor said he left the hall "humiliated and indignant that such things would be done in the name of religion". It was later reported that the bazaar had raised £4,000 for St Alban's, but the Rev Durbin said that while selling alcohol might be a short cut to financial success, it was also a "short cut to moral degradation and ruin".

The pastor's shock and disgust at what he found at the bazaar was no doubt exacerbated by the fact that earlier in the year, the Exchange Hall had been the venue for an evangelistic mission organised by the National Council of Evangelical Free Churches. The day-long event featured inspirational preachers with Bible studies and prayer meetings and according to the Methodist Times, it was well-supported by all denominations in the town, including the Leamington Road Baptists.

The other event of significance to be held at the Exchange in 1901 was a meeting of the Blackburn and District Weavers, Winders and Warpers' Association on 24th June which attracted a very large crowd, estimated at around 3,000, to protest against the "driving" system of working in the town's cotton mills. This referred to the fact that the overlookers, each of whom controlled a bank of looms, would force their operatives to keep working nonstop, and if they saw anyone pausing or attempting to take a short break they would dock their wages accordingly.

The system was particularly hard on loom workers because the overlookers themselves were paid by the mill-owners for their output and, in turn, handed out the wages to the workers under their control. Each overlooker would keep a slate on which he would record the time spent by each operative at the loom, and hence the pay they were due. The system had been blamed by the Blackburn Coroner as the cause of a young Darwen girl named McCartney committing suicide a fortnight earlier, and speakers at the meeting called for it to be ended. The association's chairman said that in his 30 years in the weaving shed he had seen how the system had crept along and it was now unbearable.

After some heated discussion, the meeting passed a resolution strongly condemning the "driving" system, saying it led to unfair competition between workers and was "disastrous" in its consequences. The resolution added: "This meeting pledges to support the Weavers' Amalgamation in its effort to abolish the slate system, the payment of overlookers' wages on the result of the weavers' earnings, and also the abolition of weavers' wage lists."

The following year, 1902, opened with Mr Nuttall and his wife putting on another free dinner for around 300 of the town's old folk, including one old lady who was said to be 98. There was no further news on any of the brewer's plans to redevelop the Exchange site, and in the meantime, the running of the hall had been left in the control of a manager, and it continued to be the venue for concerts, trade exhibitions, public meetings and bazaars, although less frequently towards the end of the decade.

Likewise, 1902 opened with no further positive news from the town council about the Blakey Moor site, despite the approval of the sub-committee's recommendations two years before. On Saturday, 22nd February, the Blackburn and District Weavers, Winders and Warpers' Association were back at the hall for a much happier event - a party to celebrate the curtailment of all-day working in the cotton mills on Saturdays, or - as the association termed it - "the twelve o'clock Saturday stop". There was a tea and concert followed by dancing, and during the evening, the association's president, George Almond, proposed a vote of thanks to the members of Parliament who had voted to introduce the measure.

On 4th October, townsfolk were invited to the Exchange to view an unusual attraction - a huge painting. Ecce Homo (Behold the Man) by Hungarian artist Mihály Munkácsy depicted the public condemnation of Christ after his arrest in Jerusalem and included 70 figures across 300ft of canvas. It was reported in the Haslingden Gazette that when it was exhibited in Budapest, the work of art had attracted 315,000 visitors. Blackburn art dealer Mr R Howarth, who was selling sixpenny tickets to the show, was presumably hoping for a tidy profit.

In the same month, the Exchange Hall was the venue for a launch party for a new evening newspaper, the Blackburn Daily Star, in which Mr Nuttall is believed to have been one of the leading shareholders. Around 150 local newsagents and their wives were invited for a supper and social and in a speech encouraging the people of Blackburn to take up the new paper, the brewery chief said no expense had been spared in their efforts to make the venture a success. Sadly, the paper was not a success and was up against the well-established Northern Daily Telegraph as well as a couple of weeklies, and it is thought that it closed after only a few issues.

Happily, the Exchange continued to thrive, and over the course of the next few years, a steady programme of meetings, concerts, bazaars, and other entertainments were booked into the hall, and silent film shows, or "electric animated pictures", as they continued to be known, became more common events. In February 1903, the classic 13-minute French science-fiction movie A Trip To The Moon topped the bill at a show which also included musical interludes and a performance by ventriloquist Bert Williams. A Trip To The Moon is recognised as one of the major landmarks in the history of cinema as it mixed animation, acting and fantasy sequences in a story about a group of astronomers who travel to the Moon after being shot out of a giant cannon.

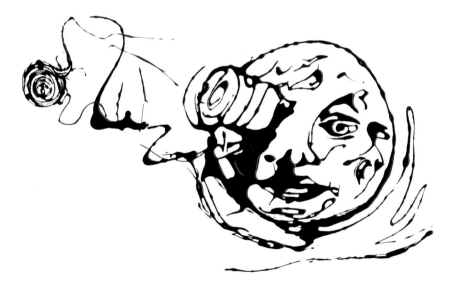

The same month, a visit by Arthur Hartley's Royal Vaudeville Company included a billtopping performance from Blackburn-born Maggie Walsh, who had gained a nationwide reputation for herself as "the Singing Mill-Girl" following a summer season in Blackpool and a run of shows in London.

In June 1904, a day-long session was staged in the Exchange by Richard Lonsdale, who described himself as a "Medical Electrician", demonstrating to members of the public - and hopefully selling - his Magnetaire Belt. He claimed that his device was "the most rational and efficacious means yet produced" for preventing, relieving and curing consumption, bronchitis, asthma, indigestion, constipation and more than a dozen other ailments of the lungs, stomach, liver and kidneys, including "all cases of paralysis, partial or total".

An advertisement published ahead of the event in the Northern Daily Telegraph quoted testimonials from customers in Burnley and Todmorden on how their Magnetaire Belt had cured various health problems including a weak heart, acute pain, rheumatism and lumbago. It is not known how many Blackburnians were convinced by his sales pitch.

The next major musical entertainment to be held at Exchange in October was something of a coup for the management when the Carl Rosa Grand Opera Company were booked for a return visit, 20 years after they had filled the hall's newly-built full-size stage for a concert on Christmas Eve, 1885. The company had grown in both size and fame in the intervening decades and in anticipation of the event, the Northern Daily Telegraph reported that the stage had undergone a major transformation to accommodate more than 100 artistes and their elaborate scenery.

# CHAPTER 13
# THE HOME OF PICTURES

**Public** meetings on various topics of the day continued to be held in the Exchange Hall, and perhaps one of the most important was on 13th February, 1905, when a local committee of female textile workers invited both men and women of the town to join their Votes for Women campaign. There was an address by Philip Snowden, the Labour Party candidate for Blackburn, and the Northern Daily Telegraph report of his speech was curiously headed: "Does the husband vote as he is told?" Mr Snowden, who was elected as the town's first Labour MP in the General Election the following year, called on the Government to introduce a bill for the enfranchisement of women without delay.

He pointed out that in the textile unions, women now formed the largest proportion of the membership and contributed more than half of all union funds, and it was only by exercising political power that women would get what they wanted. To laughter from the audience he added: "Some might say that if women had votes they would exercise them as men told them. Well, I cannot speak from personal experience, but I have heard indirectly that it is often the other way about and it is the husband who votes as he is told by his wife."

On 14th April, the politician, who was born at Cowling, near Keighley, was back at the Exchange for an evening reception with more than 500 friends and supporters following his wedding a month earlier at Otley Register Office. Blackburn's Labour Representation Committee presented the candidate and his new wife Ethel with gifts of an onyx clock, a pair of bronze -gilt vases and a 72-piece porcelain dinner service. In December the following year, the Exchange Hall staged a "Grand Demonstration" by the Votes for Women campaign chaired by Mrs Snowden, which was addressed by four of the leading members of the Suffragette movement, including Adela Pankhurst.

Two other events of note at the Exchange in 1905 occurred within a few days of each other. The Catholic Truth Society chose Blackburn for its annual conference on 25th September, and Cardinal Francis Bourne, the Archbishop of Westminster, addressed a packed hall on the subject of improving educational opportunities for Catholic children across the country.

The following week, Blackburn Corporation took over the Exchange for a week-long exhibition to mark 10 years since the opening of the town's electricity generating station in Jubilee Street - and to encourage both business and domestic consumers in the town to use electricity for lighting and power. Alderman William Thompson, chairman of the council's Electricity Committee, said that in the decade the number of consumers had risen from 40 to 1,110, boosting monthly revenue from £60 to £2,400, while the number of street lamps now using electricity instead of gas had gone up from 18 to 634.

With the exception of short films featuring Blackburn Rovers and fund-raising events for the town's cricket and football clubs, sporting occasions were rare at the Exchange. In February 1871 a billiards match had been staged between two of the greatest players of the time, John Roberts Junior and William Cook, and then in March 1906, the Assembly Hall in Town Hall Street was the venue for a three-day exhibition billiards match between the world champion W.H. Stevenson and the Irish champion, J. Duncan. It was one of a series of exhibitions around the country by the pair and there was seating for 500 for each afternoon and evening session. Billiard table manufacturers E.J. Riley Ltd of Accrington provided a special table for the match.

In the Spring of 1906, Blackburn Corporation's ongoing scheme to redevelop the Blakey Moor site was in the news again following suggested changes to the original plans. It was now being proposed by the council that a large part of the site should be devoted to a fire station, with the erection alongside of cottage homes for the firemen. As soon as the news broke, a group of concerned citizens called a public meeting at the Town Hall to object to the changes, and ahead of the gathering, an Editorial in the Northern Daily Telegraph spoke up in favour of the objectors and suggested it would be a betrayal of the town's citizens whose rates had paid for acquisition of the site to use it for a purpose which could be best placed elsewhere. Readers were reminded of the council's original plans for the development of Blakey Moor and added that the town urgently needed a public hall "suitable for large gatherings and concerts of the best class".

On 21st May, a special meeting of the town council was held to re-consider the fire station plan and there was a complete U-turn. Just a fortnight after the idea was first proposed, a resolution to defer the fire station idea and to look again at the original Blackburn Improvement Scheme - as agreed by the council in early 1900 - was passed unanimously. The Northern Daily Telegraph hailed the decision and said the council had "promptly and completely shown its respect for public opinion".

With the Blakey Moor development plans still unresolved, there was no news, either, from Alfred Nuttall about his proposal to demolish the Exchange and redevelop the site as a shopping arcade, although it must be assumed that he had lost interest in the idea. In the meantime, he had been re-elected to the town council, this time for the St Silas's Ward, which he held until early 1914, when he became an Alderman.

In September 1909, there was another attempt to drum up business with an advertisement in the Northern Daily Telegraph, stating that the "Exchange Assembly Rooms" located round the corner from the main hall on Town Hall Street were available for "private parties, public meetings etc at very reasonable terms".

As far as the main hall was concerned, what seemed to be becoming increasingly clear by this time was that its biggest value to the town in the long term could be as a cinema. In January 1909, a deal was agreed between the hall's management and Sydney Carter's New Century Pictures to stage a season of week-long programmes of silent films, interspersed with live entertainment from singers, comedians, magicians, ventriloquists and novelty acts including The Cheers and their Performing Cats and Laurie Wyle and his Mimicking Mannikin.

The programmes, which ran nightly from Monday to Saturday with afternoon matinees on Thursday and Saturday, contained a mix of dramas, comedies and documentary items, and according to regular reviews in the Northern Daily Telegraph they were very popular with townsfolk. Tickets cost one shilling, sixpence or threepence depending on your seat's distance from the screen.

Dramas on show included Wild West film The Trappers, The Diamond Thieves, The Missionary's Daughter. The Adventures of Sherlock Holmes,

Rifle Bill, A Soldier's Heroism, A Worthless Husband and The Blacksmith's Sweetheart. Documentaries screened included Earthquake In Italy, Eclipse Of The Sun and The Cotton Industry in Egypt, while When the Wife's Away, Polka On the Brain, Following in Mother's Footsteps and The Runaway Dog were among the hit comedies.

The season continued until the end of May with a couple of short breaks for the hall to stage other events, and during the run there was a special screening on one day only of The Burns-Johnson Fight, a silent film of the World Heavyweight Boxing Championship fight between Tommy Burns and Jack Johnson which was held in the open air in Sydney, Australia, on - appropriately - Boxing Day 1908. Johnson won the 14-round bout, only part of which was actually included in the two-hour film.

The film screenings were clearly a big success as Carter with his New Century Pictures was back at the Exchange only a few weeks later for another season. An advertisement in the Northern Daily Telegraph on 9th June labelled the Exchange as "the recognised home of pictures" and promised "two hours of interest and amusement nightly". The following month, the Telegraph published another advert from the Exchange: "Cinematograph operator requires pupil - thorough tuition".

# CHAPTER 14
# A NEW ERA

**In** April 1911, a notice in the Northern Daily Telegraph revealed that the Star Picture Palace Company had now taken over the management of the Exchange Hall for film screenings, promising "a new era in the annals of the Exchange" with "the latest of pictures and the best of talent". One of the biggest productions to be shown over the next few months was in the week beginning 26th June when audiences packed out the venue to watch a film of the Coronation procession of King George V, which had taken place just a few days earlier.

In September 1911, the hall was the venue for a visit by The Humanoscope, an American invention presenting "talking picture plays" which were described in promotional publicity as "a revolution in life-motion pictures". It was actually a short-lived attempt to add sound to the characters seen on silent film, with real actors hidden behind the screen and voicing the dialogue as the drama unfolded. To add to the spectacle, the programme included some sequences in which characters on screen were made to chat directly to the audience.

Another major cinema event at the Exchange that year came the following month when the main feature was The Aviator and the Journalist's Wife, a film with action aeroplane sequences, which brought moving images of flying to the people of Blackburn for the first time, just eight years after the Wright Brothers made the first powered flight in the United States and only two years after Louis Bleriot had flown a plane across the English Channel. Also in 1911, work finally got under way on the Blakey Moor development after the council decided to go ahead with the original 1900 scheme of a Public Hall, police HQ, Magistrates' Courts and council offices. With Councillor Nuttall now being a leading member of the council and in full support of the scheme, it left a big question mark over his long-term plans for the Exchange.

Early in 1912, the hall was leased to the East Lancashire Picture Company for five years at £500 a year, leaving little doubt as to its future direction, although live entertainments, public meetings and bazaars would continue to occasionally intrude on the film screenings. Towards the end of the year, there was a pause for a few weeks to allow for extensive alterations to the room, including renovations to the stage, the removal of pillars which blocked sightlines for the audience and the introduction of tip-up seats. The Exchange reopened on 23rd December with a dramatic film called The Massacre in which US troops clashed with Red Indians in the Wild West. By now, it was being advertised in the local press as "the popular picture palace" and was described as providing "the brightest and steadiest pictures in town".

Since December 1911, the Exchange Hall had faced town centre competition in attracting cinemagoers from a rival venue, the Olympia. This building opened in May 1909 in Peter Street as a roller-skating rink, but the business was not a success and it closed in November 1911, only to re-open a month later with the addition of a stage as a music hall and variety theatre. The Olympia was soon putting on film shows as well, with seating for 2,000, albeit on basic long wooden benches. It became a full-time cinema in 1921, when the benches were replaced with tip-up seats, finally closing in 1957. In the 1960s it was better known as the Locarno Ballroom, later becoming a Mecca bingo hall, and then the Golden Palms and a succession of other names as a nightclub and disco.

At this time, film shows were also being offered regularly elsewhere in the town at the Star in Little Harwood, the Victoria and the Alexandra on Eanam, the Empire at Ewood, the New King's Hall at Bank Top and occasionally also at the Central Hall in Mincing Lane.

With the council scheme to build a big new Public Hall now underway, the Corporation felt a grand gesture was needed to set the seal on the project, and Councillor Nuttall suggested that King George should be invited to Blackburn to lay the foundation stone of what was to become King George's Hall. The Royal visit was agreed for Thursday, 10th July, 1913, and with Councillor Nuttall's involvement it is probably no coincidence that plans were put in place for the Royal party to pass the Exchange en route from a visit to Roe Lee Mills via Whalley Range and Randal Street to a civic reception at the Town Hall. He arranged for a platform to be erected in front of the hall for disabled children to see the King passing, and afterwards each child was presented with a souvenir mug and invited to a special cinema show inside. The hall's windows overlooking the street were also thrown open for people to get a good view.

Unlike the big stone-laying ceremony at the Exchange in 1863, King George didn't actually visit the construction site to lay the foundation stone. Instead, after being introduced to councillors and other notables of the town, including Councillor Nuttall and his wife, the Royal visitor was handed an electric switch by the Mayor, Alderman Samuel Crossley. As the King pressed the button, a signal was given to workmen at the site to lower the stone into place, and at the same time, a flag was unfurled on the Exchange tower to signify that it had been laid.

The future of the Exchange was still a topic of conversation in the town, and earlier that year a plan for a complete remodelling of almost the entire town centre was proposed from an unusual source, Thomas Ritzema JP, the founder and proprietor of the Northern Daily Telegraph. His plan, with a detailed map, was published in his newspaper and also in the Blackburn Times, and among other things it would have involved demolition of the Market Hall on King William Street and the construction of a new covered market in Ainsworth Street.

He also proposed demolition of the Exchange and all the other properties bounded by King William Street, Sudell Cross, Northgate and Town Hall Street and their replacement with a triangular-shaped shopping arcade of about 24 shops surrounded by a glass awning in the style of the shopping arcades on Lord Street in Southport. This would be set back from Town Hall Street, doubling its width and providing a view from the Town Hall entrance to the new Magistrates Courts on Northgate.

Mr Ritzema also suggested a large equestrian statue of King Edward VII should be mounted on the corner where the Exchange Hotel stood. The proposals were laid out in an open letter to the council, and the Mayor, Alderman Crossley, said he had no objection to the plans being published, and they were "ripe for discussion". Nothing more was heard of the scheme, however, and with the First World War being imminent, Mr Ritzema did not pursue the matter.

Meanwhile, Councillor Nuttall was elected as chairman of Blackburn Conservative Party and then, newly installed as an Alderman, he was appointed Mayor of Blackburn in 1915. Unhappily, by this time he was suffering from ill-health, and as his condition worsened he had to relinquish his civic duties and moved to a nursing home in Harrogate. He died there while still the Mayor in August 1917, aged 54.

In the meantime, the East Lancashire Picture Company was suffering poor receipts for its film shows - possibly because most able-bodied men of the town were in uniform - and in August 1916 it was reported that they were thinking of giving up the lease of the hall. This apparently came to the notice of Bob Crompton, the former Blackburn Rovers and England footballer, who was now running a garage and hotel business in the town, and in November of that year he reportedly met Alderman Nuttall or his representatives and attempted to negotiate a takeover of the lease for seven years at the existing rate of £500 a year.

At the same time, it is understood that Crompton bought out the East Lancashire Picture Company for £1,200 and set up a new business, the

Exchange Picture Company Limited. He wanted the lease to be transferred to his new company, but unfortunately, Alderman Nuttall's serious illness and then death put any plans for the future of the hall on hold.

In November 1919, it was reported that a small syndicate of Blackburn businessmen were in negotiation to purchase the Exchange Hall, the hotel, and all related property in Town Hall Street for a sum of around £35,000. Surprisingly, the entire block was then put up for re-sale at a price of £70,000 - and indeed it was said that an un-named London businessman had agreed to pay that price. At the same time, it was also rumoured that the entire Exchange estate had been offered to Blackburn Corporation for a sum in excess of that figure. The Corporation apparently declined the offer, and it seems that nothing more was heard of any double-your-money London deal.

For a time, the Blackburn Wesleyan Mission, which had previously rented the former Catholic Hall (as the Church Institute) was said to be interested in that portion of the estate. But in March 1920, the Exchange Hall, related buildings, the hotel and assembly rooms were sold for an undisclosed sum to a newly-formed company, Exchange (Blackburn) Limited, which was linked to a separate concern, Olympia (Blackburn) Limited, and the registered office was named as the Olympia Theatre in Peter Street.

The change of ownership was not completed without a hitch, however. When the sale was announced, Bob Crompton claimed that under the agreement he had made with the previous owner in November 1916, he had the right of tenancy of the hall until 1923, and furthermore he should have been allowed to put in a bid to purchase the property outright before Exchange (Blackburn) Limited.

The dispute led to a three-day hearing at the Chancery Court in Manchester in June, when the new owners sought a legal declaration that the Crompton tenancy would expire in November 1920, and they also asked for an injunction to restrain him from making any bookings for films to be screened at the Exchange after that date. In his defence, the former Rovers captain told the court of an agreement with Alderman Nuttall that if the Exchange building was to be sold, it would first be offered to him. He said he already carried out structural improvements to the hall at a cost of £2,283, and he had sought and obtained permission from the owner before this work was carried out. He also said he needed to see out the terms of his seven-year tenancy to recoup the money he had spent.

The court hearing ended with the Vice-Chancellor of the County Palatine, R Lawrence KC, reserving his judgement, but it seems that he found in favour of Mr Crompton as the two parties were back in court in November, this time at the Court of Appeal in London, when Exchange (Blackburn) Limited and Alderman Nuttall's trustees sought to overturn the Vice-Chancellor's ruling that Mr Crompton had, indeed, concluded an agreement to lease the hall on the terms agreed.

After several hours of legal arguments and counter-arguments between King's Counsel representing the two sides, the Master of the Rolls, Lord Sterndale, sitting with Lord Justices Warrington and Younger, allowed the appeal. The court ruled that all Alderman Nuttall had given the ex-footballer was an assurance that if the East Lancashire Picture Company gave up the tenancy he could have it, but the details of the length of the lease had been left for subsequent negotiations, and as these had not been concluded there was no agreement to lease the premises to his private company.

The ruling cleared the way for the new owners to establish the Exchange Hall as a full-time cinema. All talk of the council or developers buying the site and demolishing the building were now dead, and in 1921, following delays caused by the war, King George's Hall was officially opened to give Blackburn the purpose-built concert hall it deserved, along with the smaller Windsor Hall for public meetings and other events.

For the next 80 years, the former Cotton Exchange was a fixture in the lives of countless thousands of Blackburnians as a picture palace under a succession of names - the Majestic, the Essoldo, the Classic, the Apollo 5 - until closure in 2005. The Grade 2-listed building lay empty for a decade, but it was bought by the Re:Source charity in September 2015, with the aim of refurbishing the hall in a £9.5million scheme to bring it back into use as a venue for exhibitions, meetings and concerts with community and work spaces and an upgraded café on the lower ground floor, plus a new mezzanine cafe/bar and a roof terrace in a space previously used for offices. But that's another story . . .

# ILLUSTRATIONS

*Figure 1:* **Queen Street Mill, Burnley**

*Source: Photography by Chris Walton*
*Published with permission: Queen Street Mill, Lancashire County Council*

An example of a working cotton mill is Queen Street Mill which opened in Burnley in 1895 as a cotton weaving mill and contained over 900 steam powered Lancashire looms. The mill closed in 1982 but was reopened in 1986 as a museum. The mill has since featured in film and television and is still open to the public with demonstrations of the looming process and steam engine.

*Figure 2:* **Competition Entry for Blackburn Cotton Exchange, 1846,
by William Haywood Brakspear and Thomas Dickson**

*Source: RIBA (Royal Institute of British Architects)
Published with permission under licence from RIBA.*

This design for Blackburn Cotton Exchange, submitted by William Hayward Brakspear and Thomas Dickson, won a £50 prize in 1846. The Blackburn Exchange Building Company intended to build the Exchange between Fleming Square and Church St. After several attempts, the plan was abandoned in 1851 after they failed to raise sufficient funds to cover the buildings costs.

*Figure 3:* **William Haywood Brakspear's design for the Cotton Exchange, 1860ish**

*Source: https://www.cottontown.org*
*Published with permision of Blackburn with Darwen Library and Information Service*

The design for the Cotton Exchange was again submitted by William Hayward Brakspear. It featured a central tower and two wings, one containing the newsroom and offices and the other the trading and performance hall. The Blackburn Exchange Company couldn't raise enough money for the whole building, so only a reduced tower and the hall were built.

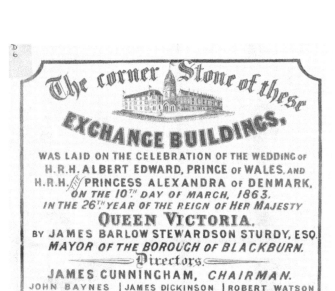

WAS LAID ON THE CELEBRATION OF THE WEDDING OF
H.R.H. ALBERT EDWARD, PRINCE OF WALES, AND
H.R.H. PRINCESS ALEXANDRA OF DENMARK,
ON THE 10TH DAY OF MARCH, 1863,
IN THE 26TH YEAR OF THE REIGN OF HER MAJESTY
QUEEN VICTORIA,
BY JAMES BARLOW STEWARDSON STURDY, ESQ.
MAYOR OF THE BOROUGH OF BLACKBURN.
Directors

JAMES CUNNINGHAM, CHAIRMAN.

| | | |
|---|---|---|
| JOHN BAYNES | JAMES DICKINSON | ROBERT WATSON |
| JOSEPH HARRISON | ABRAHAM HAWORTH | DAVID NICOL |
| EGGLES SHORROCK | JOHN SPARROW | AND |
| NATHANIEL WALSH | WILLIAM DUDLEY CODDINGTON | WILLIAM STONES. |
| THOMAS LUND | GEORGE WALMSLEY | |

SECRETARY; THOMAS CROOKE AINSWORTH,
ARCHITECT; WILLIAM HAYWARD BRACKSPEAR.
BUILDER; PATRICK FARRELL.
WILLIAM HENRY HORNBY, M.P.
JAMES PILKINGTON, M.P. } for the Borough;
GOD SAVE THE QUEEN.

*Figure 4: **Laying of the Foundation Stone, 10 March 1863***

Barely three months into the construction work, Tuesday 10th March 1863, was chosen as the day for a grand celebration to mark the laying of the new building's foundation or corner stone. It was conceived as a double celebration, as that day was also the occasion of the marriage of Queen Victoria's son, Albert Edward, Prince of Wales, to Princess Alexandra of Denmark. A public holiday had been declared, and despite the fact that the event took place during a period of economic downturn, in the midst of the Cotton Famine, when many ordinary townsfolk were struggling with poverty, a lavish ceremony and day-long festivities were organised.

Figure 5: *Ceremonial mallet and trowel used in the laying of the Exchange foundation stone*

Source: Photography by Chris Walton
Published with permission of Blackburn Museum and Art Gallery

The foundation stone of the Cotton Exchange was laid on the 10th March 1863 by Mayor James Sturdy. This silver trowel and ebony mallet were presented as gifts to the Mayor by the directors of the Blackburn Exchange Company and then used in the ceremony to place and set the Exchange foundation stone. The items are now on display in Blackburn Museum and Art Gallery.

*Figure 6:* **Painting of the laying of the Exchange Foundation Stone by Vladimir Sherwood, 1863**

*Source: Blackburn Museum and Art Gallery*
*Published with permission of Blackburn Museum and Art Gallery.*

This painting by Vladimir Osipovich Sherwood shows the laying of the Exchange foundation stone on the 10th March 1863. The day was chosen to celebrate the Royal wedding of Prince Albert and Princess Alexandra and was attended by all the town, including dignitaries such as the Mayor and the Feilden family. This painting was on display in the Exchange Hall for a number of years before being lost. It was rediscovered in the 1960s in the Technical School building and is now on display at Blackburn Museum and Art Gallery.

*Figure 7: **Exchange building in its early form***

*Source: https://cottontown.org*
*Published with permission from Blackburn with Darwen Library*
*and Information Service*

The Exchange building shown soon after opening, thought to be in the 1870s. The central tower originally had a flat roof as a shortage of funds meant the original plans had to be scaled back. Later alterations increased the height of the tower roof and removed the entrance steps. During this time, the hall was used as a newsroom, for cotton trading and as a performance hall.

*Figure 8: **Program for the opening concert of the Exchange, 1865***

*Source: Blackburn Library*
*Published with permission from Blackburn with Darwen Library and Information Service*

The new Exchange Hall was designed so that the space could be used as a performance hall as well as trading. This was put to use with a grand concert to celebrate the building opening on the 26th April 1865. The concert was headlined by opera singer Euphrosyne Parepa and featured a full orchestra playing pieces such as the William Tell Overture and I Dreamt I Dwelt in Marble Halls. The evening was well received, with performers receiving cheers and applause from the audience.

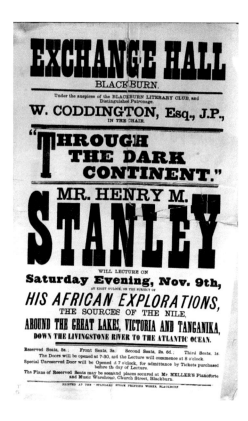

*Figure 9:* **Poster for a talk by Henry Stanley on his African expedition**

*Source: Blackburn Library*
*Published with permission from Blackburn with Darwen Library and Information Service*

The Exchange Hall and Assembly rooms hosted many guest speakers including politicians, religious leaders, writers and explorers. This poster advertises a lecture and photos by the explorer Henry Stanley from November 1878 following his expedition across central Africa. Other famous speakers who visited the Exchange included author Charles Dickens in 1869 who read from his story, A Christmas Carol, and suffragette Adela Pankhurst in 1906 who was campaigning for women's rights.

Figure 10: **Exterior of the Exchange, 1909**

*Source: Blackburn Library*
*Published with permission of Blackburn with Darwen Library and Information Services*

Many building changes occurred at the Exchange as it was repurposed to a performance hall and then cinema. By the early 20th century, the central tower's peaked roof had been completed and inside, modern electric lighting was fitted, a larger stage would be built, along with balconies and folding seats to accommodate larger audiences for films and performances as the owners tried to keep up with competing venues.

*Figure 11:* **Opening of the Coronation Bazaar at the Exchange, 1911**

*Source: Blackburn Weekly Telegraph 11th March 1911 (Blackburn Library)*
*Published with permission of Blackburn with Darwen Library and Information Service*

For many years, the Exchange was host to a number of grand bazaars - charity events with market stalls, food, drink, games and entertainment, held to raise money for local organisations. The Grand Venetian Bazaar, for example, was held in 1885 to raise funds for St Matthews Church and saw The Exchange decorated with paintings of the canals and buildings of Venice. Blackburn Rovers also held a bazaar in 1895 in an attempt to raise enough money to pay off the debt incurred in buying their new grounds at Ewood Park.

# POSTSCRIPT

**The** journey of purchasing and starting to refurbish The Exchange has been exhilarating and exhausting in equal measure. When we started what was to become Re:Ignite Church in 2012, we knew we were meant to buy this building for the town. There it was, one of the most stunning and significant buildings in the town, going to ruin. As well as horrendous dry rot, there were pigeons and rats everywhere and a tree growing out of the roof. The previous owners had rebuffed all attempts to find a solution or even to sell the building, so it had been unoccupied, empty for 10 years since the Apollo Cinema closed.

Putting it simply, we were sure that God wanted us to buy the building even though we would need more than £6 million to restore it, so started a charity, Re:Source Blackburn in 2013 to buy it. We were sure that we should pay £550,000 for it even though the owner wanted more than twice that. After a year of negotiation during which we had received a generous donation of £500,000 from the Lancaster Foundation, the owners agreed to sell it for that amount, to the astonishment of the Council and all concerned, in September 2015.

It has always been our intention to see this beautiful building restored and continue to cause a gasp of wonder as people walk upstairs and see this remarkable, awe-inspiring space. We want to see hope restored in our town and believe that this building can play a significant part in that. We're so excited to be bringing The Exchange back into sustainable use as a vibrant and diverse venue and to fulfil our dream to deliver activities that inspire hope, creativity, and excellence for everyone.

The journey would not have been possible without the 13 intrepid original members of the church who were willing to take such a risk, or without the £120,000 loan from Cornerstone Practice to cover the VAT on the building. We could never have achieved so much without Re:Ignite continuing to cover much of the running costs, without outstanding support from BwD Council and without the countless volunteers who have cleaned, painted, donated and supported some amazing community events. We are grateful for financial support from so many funders, particularly the Architectural Heritage Fund, the National Lottery Heritage Fund and Blackburn with Darwen Borough Council.

Other than the enormous painting in Blackburn Museum of the laying of the foundation stone in 1864, we had little idea of the history of the building before it became a cinema in the 1920s other than snippets and headlines. I am delighted that, thanks to the incredible work of the authors and other volunteers, we now have this book on the history of the building before it became a cinema. Thank you.

**Dr Alastair Murdoch**

*Founding trustee, Re:Source & Re:Ignite Church*

# FURTHER RESEARCH

If you are interested in finding out more about Lancashire's cotton industry you may find the following references and resources useful.

### Blackburn Central Library

Blackburn Central Library, Town Hall St, Blackburn BB2 1AG

Blackburn Central Library holds the borough's main local studies collections including: books and trade directories birth, marriage and death indexes, cemetery records census returns, ephemera and broadsheets, maps, newspapers dating back over 200 years, photographs, special collections.

### Cottontown.org

https://www.Cottontown.org/

A resource developed and maintained by Blackburn with Darwen Library and Information Service. Cottontown.org charts the rise and decline of the cotton industry and its impact on the community and a wider social history of the area. It comprises images, print resources, maps and broadsheets digitised from the historical archives held in the library and museum.

## Blackburn Museum

Blackburn Museum & Art Gallery, Museum Street, Blackburn BB1 7AJ

Blackburn Museum's local history section includes the collection from the former Lewis Textile Museum including the gallery which houses the collection of looms renamed Cottontown. The Lewis Textile Museum was bequeathed by Thomas Boys Lewis, a local cotton industrialist.

## Helmshore Museum

Helmshore Mills Textile Museum, Holcombe Road, Helmshore, Rossendale BB4 4NP.

Helmshore museum consists of two historic working mills: Higher Mill a wool-fulling mill and Whitaker Mill a cotton mill.

## Queen Street Mill

Queen Street Mill Textile Museum, Queen Street, Harle Syke Burnley, Lancashire BB10 2HX

Queen Street Mill is the last surviving 19th century steam powered weaving mill in the world.

## Manchester Exchange

Royal Exchange Theatre, St Ann's Square, Manchester M2 7D

Manchester's Royal Exchange theatre is an iconic, spaceship-like theatre-in-the-round housed within the original Great Hall of the stunning Grade II listed building built in the 1800s as the Manchester Exchange. Though it wasn't the first Exchange, in fact, it's the third! The website contains a detailed history of the Exchange and the building is open to visitors who can see the magnificent columns and stunning glass domes of the original building.

**Lancashire Archives**

Lancashire Record Office, Bow Lane, Preston PR1 2RE

Lancashire County Council's archive service has unique and irreplaceable archives, records and local history resources from area, made available for exploring personal, family or community history. This includes the Lancashire Sound Collections, an extensive collection of recordings and oral history interviews covering the local authorities of Lancashire, Blackburn with Darwen and Blackpool.